GET *F.I.T.* GO FAR!

15 THINGS LEADERS ABSOLUTELY MUST DO TO INCREASE ORGANIZATIONAL PERFORMANCE

BY HERKY CUTLER

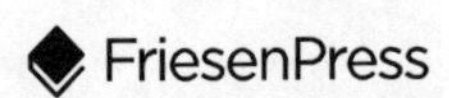

Suite 300 - 990 Fort St
Victoria, BC, Canada, V8V 3K2
www.friesenpress.com

First Edition — 2016

Editor, Coach: Gordon Thomas
Editor: Kim Rempel

ISBN
978-1-4602-7685-3 (Hardcover)
978-1-4602-7686-0 (Paperback)
978-1-4602-7687-7 (eBook)

1. Business & Economics, Organizational Behavior

Distributed to the trade by The Ingram Book Company

I'm inspired - I love the energy, the straightforwardness, and the tips. I know *Get **F.I.T.** Go Far!* will be one of the few business books that I'll keep on my bookshelf and turn back to time and again. Written for the busy manager or executive, this book is easy to skim, but organized so that help for specific problems can quickly be found, right when you need it!

I was personally impressed by Herky's holistic approach to leadership, from looking at the inner lives and personal characteristics of leaders to the differences between the written and unwritten values of organizations. I appreciated the level of detail in his stories and how he integrated key facts from other respected authors with reports of his own action research projects. Herky isn't just sharing what he believes to be true; rather, he has grounded many of those beliefs in the existing literature and confirmed some of them with original research.

There are practical tips, tools, and tests throughout the book, along with inspiring quotes. Herky also includes stories from working in schools, small and medium-sized organizations, government-run organizations, and large multinationals. There is something in this book for every leader.

Herky has much to teach us about how to lead our organizations more effectively.

-Dr. Roberta Neault, CCC, CCDP, GCDFi
President, Life Strategies Ltd. Associate Dean, Faculty of Behavioural Sciences, Yorkville University

Herky Cutler's *Get F.I.T. Go Far!* is a self-exploratory, organizational assessment and improvement, and team leadership book all wrapped up in one. This book is for you if you are ready to assess yourself, your team, your workplace, and are ready to make daring changes. You will be inspired to make fearless and informed decisions that will "help move the organization forward, build staff cohesiveness and foster outstanding customer service."

Get F.I.T. Go Far! is filled with dozens of examples that illustrate what any leader can and must do to drive organizational performance. Better yet, the comfortable, casual writing style of Herky Cutler allows his many years of experience to come together in a way that is both delightful to read and deep in wisdom. Whether you are new to your leadership role, carry years of leadership experience with you or are just curious about what it's like to be a leader, you are guaranteed to find some gems that will make you glad you picked up this book!

-David Gouthro, CSP,
professional facilitator, provocateur

There is always pressure on teams and organizations to perform and maximize profits and there are countless books on the subject. Herky's book addresses a much more important issue...the health and fitness of the group and how vital that is to success. I love that it's written with a focus on the person not just profits because they are the most important cog in the machinery.

-Alvin Law,
Hall of Fame speaker, storyteller, motivational rabble-rouser and author of *Alvin's Laws of Life: 5 Steps to Overcome Anything*

From analyzing your organization's effectiveness, to uncovering blind spots, to developing inner grit to strategizing changes for growth and effectiveness, Cutler shows the way and offers simple, yet effective tools. Give your perspective on organizational functioning an overall and tune-up by reading *Get F.I.T. Go Far!*

-Patricia Morgan MA CCC
professional speaker, therapeutic counsellor, resiliency expert
and author of *From Woe To Wow: How Resilient Women Succeed at Work*

There is no shortage of books that purport to provide the answers to the problems ailing organizations today, many of which are filled with theoretical, abstract concepts too difficult to implement. I found that *Get F.I.T. Go Far!* is not one of those books. I appreciate that Herky is a proponent of real-world recommendations that individuals and organizations can put into practice. He has drawn on his many years of experience in varied circumstances to create an easy-to-read book that provides practical advice for leaders interested in effecting change.

-Dana Terry, Deputy Chief
Lethbridge Fire and Emergency Services

I absolutely enjoyed reading this book! The 'real' speak is refreshing and Herky Cutler delivers it in a genuinely caring fashion. The content is thought provoking and hits the key strategies that leaders need to contemplate and execute to be effective. As a training provider/organizer, Herky's book opened my eyes and provided me insight to better understand what drives a leader and how leaders can impact their organization's success. *Get F.I.T. Go Far!* is a paramount read that will create a springboard for anyone in a leadership role or aspiring to be. Get ready, to get real!

-**Franca Best**, Program Development Supervisor
Calgary Board of Education

Herky provides a unique perspective on organizational fitness. He leverages a wealth of personal experiences to provide plenty of anecdotal material to support his insights. This not only gives credibility to his ideas, it also makes the book an interesting and easy read. He has provided a wealth of information and tools that you can use to make and keep your organization more ***F.I.T.*** The book can easily serve as a manager's handbook. Each chapter tackles a different aspect of organizational fitness that can be referred to individually as often as required. If you are in a leadership role; team leader, manager, supervisor, senior executive this book is a 'must' to have and read.

-**Joel Sweeney**,
Owner and Founder of *Professionally Speaking* and author of *The Speaker's Tool Box*

Contents

This book is dedicated to the memories of my father, Harry Cutler, my brother, Errol Cutler, and my sister, Mona Ravvin. Your spirits live on in me and I have taken your gifts and shared them with the world. I love you. To my mother Rosie, who died recently at the age of 99.5, thanks for trying to hold on to see this book Mom. I love you too!

Acknowledgements

It's been a long road to the end of this, my first book. I always knew I wanted to write one, but I wasn't sure it would ever happen. I'm very grateful that it has. The work that I do with organizations is rewarding because I see both people and organizations implement change. To be able to take what I've learned by watching, listening, asking questions, and then compiling those experiences into this book, has been a joy.

Organizational Fitness is a concept that has been around for a while, and it's growing ever more popular. I believe organizational leaders intuitively know if their teams, departments, or companies are fit or not. They may not be able to articulate exactly what isn't right, but I think they feel it on some level. I'm thrilled to offer this book as a tool to help these organizations identify and correct such issues, and help guide them toward overall fitness.

This project didn't happen through my efforts alone though, that's for sure. First, I want to thank my book coach, Les Kletke, who created a structure that helped me focus my writing and critique it from the point of view of the reader. Thank you to fellow speakers Michelle Ray and Joel Sweeney, who generously shared their knowledge and experience from writing their own books. Your advice was invaluable.

Thank you to those who took time out of their busy schedules to read a chapter of the book and offer some great feedback that, in many cases, shifted the whole context of the chapter: Toyese Sanni, Paula Wischoff Yerama, Peter Temple, Tina Varughese, Tony Fisher, Quinton Crow Shoe, Brian Lee, Patricia Morgan, Alvin Law, David Saxby, Dave Redekopp, Les Morgan, Wayne Mann and Lana Bullough, I am very grateful to you.

To one of my editors, Kim Rempel, thank you for having the courage to slash and burn my rambling and redundancy. It helped make the book so much smoother to read. To my other editor and coach Gordon Thomas, thank you for your insight, wisdom, and support on this project. Your experience and kindness are greatly appreciated.

To the folks at Friesen Press, thank you for assembling this manuscript in a professional manner, and for creating a product that I can be proud of.

Finally, to the one person that put up with me through every facet of this experience, my wife Riesah Prock, I thank you from the bottom of my heart. I didn't always agree with your advice, or point of view, but I'm so grateful that you care enough to offer them. Thank you for your encouragement, patience, and never-ending belief in me. I love you Honey.

Introduction

Why Write this Book?

Organizations are an integral aspect of this society. When you think about it, they haven't been around all that long compared to how long humans have been here. Organizations are products, protectors, and predictors of civilization. Where would we be in this day and age without them? How will they shape our future?

Organizations help us establish and maintain law and order, advocate and care for the sick and needy, and provide us with the goods and services we use every single day. As the world continues to grow, the role organizations play will become even more important. Helping organizations become better at what they do then, is important work, and I'm blessed to do it.

Who Should Read it?

This book can help any kind of organization, whether for profit, or not for profit. Whether a large-scale company, or a modest start-up. At the heart of every organization is the leadership group, and this book is for all you managers, supervisors, team leaders and CEOs out there. You are integral to the fitness of your organization. You are the decision makers, visionaries, and role models. Without you, there is no direction, identity, or purpose for existing.

For some of you, what I share in the book may not be new. Hopefully though, you will be reminded of things that are already working in your organization, or of things that you might now see fit to incorporate. Take action and see what comes of it. You may be pleasantly surprised.

For others, what I share with you will be new information. Use these tools and insights in whatever way you can to make your organization better for you, your staff and your customers. Take a risk and try something different.

What I Hope for

Change. I hope that from reading this book you will change, even in some small way. I hope you'll find something in here that speaks to you, and that you will bring it to your organization so that it will change too. I hope that your organization will become more fit, more dynamic, and more integral than it already is. I hope your organization is among those who lead our civilization into the future.

CHAPTER ONE

Evaluate Your Fitness Quotient

The Organizational Fitness Test

Mirror, Mirror, on the Wall

When you look in the mirror, do you see a fit, upbeat risk taker who embraces change and loves to learn? Perhaps you see someone who has become a little out of shape, tired, and less willing to change. If you don't like what you see, what are you prepared to do about it?

Organizations, like people, are organic entities in a state of constant flux. They can be out of shape, incredibly fit, or somewhere in between. When was the last time you looked into the mirror of your organization? Did you see a vibrant culture with enthusiastic employees, or a stagnant organization that has difficulty adapting to change?

"Organizational ***FIT***ness" is a state of being for your organization. It is the degree to which your organization is doing well in a variety of areas, from culture and strategic planning, to staff relationships and customer service. This book is about helping organizations take action and create a level of ***FIT***ness that you are excited about, and that will keep your organization healthy for years to come.

Organizational FITness is the degree to which your organization is doing well in a variety of areas, from culture and strategic planning, to staff relationships and customer services.

F.I.T. stands for "Future," "Identity," and "Team."

Future: What the organization is doing now to prepare for the future.

There are a number of questions to consider when planning for the future. What is the vision for this organization? What strategic plan will guide the organization into the future? Is there a career development program in place for staff so that every employee has goals and objectives they are working toward, whether they stay in the organization long term or not? How does the organization develop leaders from within, so that succession planning happens smoothly and in a timely fashion?

Identity: How the organization is perceived by others, including employees, competitors and customers.

Can you describe what your organizational culture is? Does your organization have a clear mission statement and does everybody actually know what it is? What are your organization's core values? How do those values translate into day-to-day operations? How are staff and customers treated? Are your customers recommending your organization to their family and friends?

Team: How well your team functions.

What's the level of trust between management and staff? What's the level of trust between staff and customers? How well do your team members get along with each other? How do you manage multi-generational issues in your workplace? Is your team as productive as they can be? Is customer service recognized as the number one priority for your team?

I realize I've given you a lot of questions in this section. But if you don't ask them, you won't get the answers that could make a huge difference in your organizational performance.

So how does your organization stack up? Take this test and find out.

The Organizational Fitness Test ©

Rate the following statements by putting a number between 1-10 in the blank next to each statement, with 1 representing the *lowest* rating and 10 the *highest*. Add up the ratings and place your total at the bottom of the page.

______ Our organization has a great strategic plan to prepare us for the future.

______ There is a career development program in place, so staff know what career goals they are working toward, both within the company, and beyond.

______ Our organization has a program in place to develop leaders for the future.

______ Job descriptions are well defined, so there is no confusion as to what staff are expected to do.

______ Our organization knows its mission and operates with a set of values that demonstrate that mission. Most of the staff know and support these values.

______ The communication in our organization is clear and consistent at all levels.

______ The vast majority of our customers would recommend us to others.

______ Our team is as productive as it can be.

______ Staff in our organization are engaged in their work most of the time.

______ Staff and management see eye-to-eye in our organization.

______ Great customer service is the number one goal of every employee in our organization.

______ Our team members get along well with one other.

Total Score = ____/120

How did you do?

If you scored;

110 – 120 Top of Your Game

Congratulations! Your organization seems to be working well. If adjustments are needed, they'll be minor. You should be very proud!

96 – 109 Rolling Along

Most of the areas in your organization are in pretty good shape. You may want to use a consultant to help you focus on improving the fitness level in one or two areas.

81 - 95 On the Right Path

Some areas in your organization are probably working well while others are not. A consultant is recommended to work with your company over a short period of time to get you back on track.

71 - 80 Fork in the Road

This doesn't necessarily mean that your organization is new, but it operates as if it were. Your organization may be at a crossroads, and what you do at this point will determine future success. A consultant is recommended to work with you on an ongoing basis to help move your organization forward.

70 or less Are Your Funeral Arrangements in Place?

Your company is dying! I'm guessing there are all sorts of issues and problems that need to be addressed in your organization. You would definitely benefit from having a consultant work with your company over an extended period of time.

Take Action - There's No Time Like the Present

So what now? Well, of course no organization is perfect, and this test is merely a guideline to get you thinking a little more deeply about what's actually going on in yours. Use the results of this test as a planning tool instead of a report card. Every organization has some good things going for it, and areas that need work. Where you scored high reveals where your organizational strengths lie. Conversely, you can also see which areas need improvement.

The challenge is to do something about it. A lot of organizations don't do anything about their situation, even when they've asked the kinds of questions that are in the fitness test. Don't be one of those organizations.

Once you've decided to take action, the next step is to determine what area of your organization to work on. The natural tendency may be to pick one of the areas of weakness to work on. This may not be the best decision. In their book, *First, Break All The Rules,* Curt Coffman and Marcus Buckingham discuss this tendency. Their research with some of America's most successful companies indicates that leaders of these companies often choose to invest time and money into developing strengths, not working on weaknesses.

A friend used a baseball analogy when we were discussing this concept. Is a greater impact produced by helping a ballplayer improve his batting average to the point where the difference could land him in the Baseball Hall of Fame, or should he spend that same time improving his less than mediocre fielding?

The answer is not obvious. Improving a batting average and getting into the Hall of Fame may be a great individual accomplishment, but it may not help the team as much as if this player became a great fielder. You can't win baseball games if your opponent is putting more men on base and scoring more runs than you do.

In your organization, it makes sense then to determine what gives you the most overall benefit in terms of investing time, energy and money into moving it forward. It may be a combination of working on a strength and a weakness simultaneously. Every organization is different. If I were consulting with you, we would develop a customized plan based on the resources you have, and would investigate which aspect of ***F.I.T.*** would make sense to address first.

This book is divided into three sections; Future, Identity and Team, and it is filled with tips, tricks and stories about how to help your organization Get ***F.I.T.***, and Go Far!

FUTURE

"The past cannot be changed.
The future is yet in your power."

-Mary Pickford

What the organization is doing now to prepare for the future

CHAPTER TWO

Use Chaos and Change to Gain a Leading Edge

Change isn't Good or Bad, it Just is

"Every successful organization has to make the transition from a world defined primarily by repetition to one primarily defined by change. This is the biggest transformation in the structure of how humans work together since the Agricultural Revolution."

-Bill Drayton

Ch-Ch-Changes, Turn and Face the Strange Ch-Ch-Changes -David Bowie

One of the most important aspects of planning for the future is expecting and dealing with change.

It was a typical day in Montreal when the phone rang. I picked it up, said hello, and heard my grandmother say, "So you don't have a father anymore." My dad, Harry, who had come back to the city for a brief vacation, died of a heart attack in his sleep at the age of 55. I was 19 at the time, and my life changed forever.

We all deal with change in our lives, some of us better than others. Change comes in many different forms; loss of a job, end of a relationship, grieving over something or someone, natural phenomena, war. Changes happen to us directly or indirectly. They require us to respond - to do things differently or to adjust our way of thinking. Change is inevitable and chaotic, impermanence is a reality we live with as human beings, like it or not.

We can also initiate change. This requires a whole different set of skills and a different mindset. Initiating change is a proactive approach, which requires diligence and hard work. We have to do something to make the change happen. We've all initiated change in our lives at some point in time haven't we? We've begun diets and fitness programs, initiated relationships or taken new jobs. We've learned new things or taken up hobbies. Usually, we initiate change in our lives to make things better.

When was the last time you initiated a significant change in your life? How successful were you in making that change a permanent part of your life? Many people try to initiate change but aren't always successful. In my own life, I've started countless diets and I'm still not happy with my weight. I quit smoking a hundred times before I was finally successful, and I still have great difficulty eating well while traveling. Change isn't easy.

What gets in the way of change? Fear is a big factor, not only fear of failure, but fear of success. It's more comfortable staying where we are, even if where we are is not where we want to be. Lack of support is another. It's much harder making big changes alone, so having a support system can really help. Sometimes resources are lacking and that can also affect one's ability to make changes. And let's face it, some people just don't give a damn, and don't want to change.

Change will occur in your organization, whether you like it or not. How you adapt, prepare for, embrace or reject it, is the key to a successful organization. When was the last time you experienced or initiated significant change in your organization? What was that like for you?

It's Alive! So You Need to Feed it

Your body is a living organism, and so is your organization. As long as it is comprised of, and does business with people, it is alive. Arie de Geus, in his book *The Living Company* says, "All companies exhibit the behavior and certain characteristics of living entities. All companies learn. All companies, whether explicitly or not, have an identity that determines their coherence. All companies build relationships with other entities, and all companies grow and develop until they die."

Unless you continue to breathe life into your organization, it *will* die. Each of these major corporations—Enron, Compaq, General Foods, TWA, Eastern Airlines, Woolworth's, Kodak, T. Eaton Company, Blockbuster Video, and Standard Oil—is no longer with us. The ability of an organization to cope with, adapt to, and thrive during periods of change is critical to the survival of that organization.

De Geus also talks about the longevity of organizations, and says that the average life expectancy of a multinational Fortune 500 company is somewhere between 40-50 years, much less than the average life expectancy of a human being. Yet, there are corporations that have been around for hundreds of years, more than 5,000 of them over 200 years old. The potential for long-lasting organizations is there, but for some reason, most of our corporations never reach their potential. Why is that?

According to de Geus, "Companies die because their managers focus on the economic activity of producing goods and services, and they forget that their organizations' true nature is that of a community of humans." It's about how organizations learn, interact with other entities and how they treat the humans that work for and with them. It's really about how organizations deal with change.

"Companies die because their managers focus on economic activity of producing goods and services, and they forget that their organizations' true nature is that of a community of humans."
-Arie de Geus

Integrity is More Important than Winning

I had the privilege of working on a friend's mayoral campaign, which was a wonderful example of this phenomenon. I was studying organizational behavior in graduate school at the time, and wrote a paper comparing a political campaign to an organization, and how both are living organisms that need to adapt to change.

Running a campaign to become mayor is a microcosm of any organization, the major difference being that a campaign has a designated start and end point. It's simply an accelerated version of an organization. When you think about it, a campaign is an organization. You need people to run it, a location to house it, a purpose for existing, a CEO, a business plan, a marketing program, a budget, a product or service that is being sold, and customers.

In this case, the candidate was the CEO, the purpose was to get that candidate elected as mayor, the product was the candidate's political savvy, experience, and ability to run a major Canadian city, the business plan was the candidate's platform, the marketing program was the way in which the candidate and the platform were presented to the public, and the customers were the citizens of that city. Every aspect that exists in an organization existed in this campaign, but we only had three months to get this organization established and successful.

How do you manage such an organization? How do you plan for the inevitable changes that will occur in a short lifespan? In retrospect, I'm not sure we had a plan to handle contingencies, but there was a spirit at campaign headquarters, instilled in us by the candidate, that had us believing we could handle anything. We felt we were doing the right thing. We believed in what the candidate stood for, and when you believe in something with passion, it's a lot easier to sell your product or service. It's about the "why" and not the "what" of the organization (I talk more about this in Chapter Nine).

We rolled out the business plan and marketing program and, in a political environment, feedback is relatively immediate. Public opinion polls determined the course of the campaign, indicating we were either on the right track with our customers or needed to adapt our message.

I remember a poll indicating we were losing ground. We called an emergency meeting to discuss how to handle this change. We talked about focusing on more controversial issues. We talked about campaigning to different neighborhoods more aggressively than originally anticipated. We were modifying the strategy in real time, embracing the change and moving boldly ahead.

With every successful strategic move reflected in the polls by a gain in customer support, there were cheers at campaign headquarters, smiles on everyone's faces, and elevated confidence that we were doing the right thing. Conversely, with every drop in the polls, there was another emergency meeting and another scramble to change direction to stay competitive with the other candidates. We laughed. We cried.

I learned that in a tight political race with much at stake, sometimes the going gets tough, the gloves come off, and fair fighting goes out the window. Does that sound familiar in the context of organizations and capitalist western culture? In the campaign, it became difficult to distinguish between who was promising to do what, and who could deliver on their promise. It was moving into the realm of personality. Things got dirty.

This could be a defining moment in the life of a person, a political campaign, or an organization. My candidate told us, "I refuse to play dirty, refuse to make personal comments about other candidates, and refuse to get caught up in those kinds of tactics." Our candidate remained ethically strong, even when it might have cost us the election.

My candidate did the right thing without compromising values, ethics, and the vision that brought us all on board in the first place. Our mayoral campaign was an organization we were proud of. Were we successful? Well, we didn't win, so we didn't reach our goal. On the other hand, we felt victorious because we all walked away from that experience feeling good about ourselves and our organization. There are numerous examples of organizations that have failed and died because they had no platform they were willing to stand by no matter what. They lacked integrity and were deemed to be unethical.

Enron is perhaps the most famous example of all. Once the seventh largest company in the United States, it came tumbling down in 2001 due to unethical practices on the part of both internal executives and external banks and advisors. Sixteen of those executives were sentenced to prison.

On the other side of the ethical coin, there are also many examples of ethical corporations that have remained strong and vibrant for many years. L'Oreal, considered to be the world's leading cosmetic company, is one of these corporations. L'Oreal has been around for over a century, operating in 130 countries and generating over 20 billion euros in sales in 2011. In 2012, L'Oreal was chosen to be one of *The World's Most Ethical Companies®* for the third time in six years.

The story of the mayoral campaign is a perfect example of how organizations must deal with change, and make decisions quickly sometimes. Change is inevitable, so the lesson is in how one prepares for, and meets change. Some people consider change to be bad. Others describe it as something good. Personally, I see change as neither good nor bad: change simply *is*.

How You Respond to Change Makes it Good or Bad

Organizations need to expect change,
embrace it, and, more importantly,
look for the opportunity within it.

I recall seeing a YouTube video after the devastating tsunami that hit Japan in 2011.

People came together in that country and remained calm. There was no rioting, no looting, and no sense of panic. People helped each other get food and supplies, supported each other, and began the rebuilding process. Whether change is good or bad is in the eye of the beholder. Eckhart Tolle captures this notion beautifully in his quote, "*Some changes look negative on the surface but you will soon realize that space is being created in your life for something new to emerge.*"

Organizations need to expect change, embrace it and, more importantly, look for the opportunity within it. You can take steps to strategically anticipate change. Here are some questions to consider that can get you started.

- Are your customers happy with your organization?
- What are your customers telling your staff about the business?
- Are staff bringing the feedback from the customer back to you?
- Are you open to receiving that feedback from the customer or staff member?
- Are there things going on in the world that will affect how customers use your products or services?
- What kinds of technologies are on the horizon to help your organization grow and customers engage with you?
- Are there new competitors emerging in your industry?
- How will you deal with them?

Staying in touch with the ever-changing corporate environment and understanding how your customers use your products or services is paramount. Listening to customer feedback and incorporating it into the existing operation is mandatory for survival. If you truly understand this, you can adapt to changes that may affect customer satisfaction by continually giving them what they need and want.

Anticipate Change. Be Proactive. No Need to Wait for Change to Happen

You can also initiate change to seamlessly improve customers' experience and satisfaction. A perfect example of this is the twelve-year blockbuster deal signed between Rogers Telecommunications and the National Hockey League early in 2014. While the deal may spell the end of one of Canada's oldest traditions, *Hockey Night In Canada*, it illustrates Rogers' understanding of the appetite Canadians have for the game of hockey.

The new deal will see more hockey coverage on more platforms with more consumer choice. How long do you think it will take before Canadians forget about *Hockey Night In Canada*? This is a bold move initiated by an organization who paid more than five billion dollars to change the way customers engage with hockey and provide them with something they didn't even know they wanted.

Here are eight tips for your organization to thrive through change:

Be prepared

Change is going to happen, so always be ready for it. Expect it and it will be easier to cope with. Training staff to be prepared will also help minimize surprise and fear.

Ask for staff and customer feedback

Your staff and customers will tell you if things are going well, and when they're not. When you know about issues, you can resolve them. Sailing along without regularly checking in with your staff and customers can keep you in the dark.

Keep on top of your competition

Some organizations tend to just mind their own business. They believe that taking care of their own organization is the most important thing and they don't worry about what other organizations are doing. This is a mistake. Pay attention to what your competitors are doing and adjust accordingly.

Talk about threats

In staff meetings, incorporate a regular dialogue on what things in the world pose threats to your organization. This includes things like economic shifts, competition, technology, shifting demographics and available manpower.

Communication

When changes are occurring in your organization, keep the lines of communication open. Let everyone know what's going on.

Leadership training

The more people you have within your organization who have great leadership skills, the easier it will be to cope with and thrive through change. Leaders expect change and are ready to adapt.

Re-visit the strategic plan

Just as organizations are living organisms, strategic plans should be as well. Just because they may have been designed initially during times of change these strategic plans need to be modified. Goals and objectives need to adjust for the change.

Stay positive

There's nothing more important during times of change than a calm, positive, and focused leader. Humans don't deal with stress very well when their emotions are high and their thoughts are negative.

Change is inevitable, and the success of your organization will depend on your attitude towards it. In the context of organizational fitness, the more comfortable and creative you become with change, the more fit your organization will be. So Get *F.I.T.,* and Go Far!

CHAPTER THREE

Two Missing Ingredients for Developing Top-Notch Strategic Plans

Everyone Needs to Be Heard

"Without strategy, execution is aimless. Without execution, strategy is useless."

-Morris Chang

If You Don't Have Buy-In, Be Prepared for Sabotage

The future of any organization depends upon the ability of its leaders to develop a strategic plan.

Does your organization have one? If so, is your strategic plan successful? Is each individual within your organization working to her potential to help make the plan succeed? If individuals aren't being as productive and efficient as they can be, chances are the organization as a whole is lacking. There could be a host of reasons for this, including the quality of leadership or employees, a corporate culture that isn't conducive to productivity, or a poor overall strategic plan. This chapter is about why you should have a plan, and how to make it a great one.

Posted by Shyama Shankar in Management Guru, Mar. 24, 2014

In an effective strategic plan, everything revolves around a mission statement, as illustrated in Shyama Shankar's Strategic Planning Cycle. Management and staff work together to establish goals, prioritize tasks, develop strategies, and determine expected outcomes. This all sounds good, doesn't it? So why doesn't every organization do it? And of those who do, why do many implement their strategy poorly? It boils down to one thing; total buy-in from each staff member.

If the entire staff isn't on board, the plan will likely fail. There will be overt and covert attempts to sabotage. Those who don't buy in won't give a damn, doing just enough to keep their jobs.

I've witnessed this sort of activity as a staff member many times. The result is rarely satisfying.

Does your staff buy in? Here's a test for you, one that I've developed and used a number of times with success. If you have a strategic plan or mission statement, have someone come into your organization and ask staff, off the cuff, what that statement is. My experience has shown that, unless a strategic planning exercise was done that week, only a minuscule percentage of staff can tell you what it is. Few will know it, and fewer will believe it.

What's happening here is that management (good intentions notwithstanding) is trying to develop an organizational strategy to move the company forward. But they become impatient. Instead of making sure that everyone is in total agreement with the strategic plan and attendant mission statement, they dismiss those who are in disagreement, and produce the strategic plan anyway.

That's a big mistake! I've seen staff go through the motions of a strategic planning exercise because they assume they know what the outcome will be. They know that management is only interested in the *illusion* of a strategic plan that everyone will follow. The illusion gives them a feeling of accomplishment, but it isn't received and believed in by the staff. Even if one member dissents, the process should be stopped. That staff person needs to be heard. When one person in a group is feeling something, chances are others are feeling it too. The time and patience needed to get everyone on board is well worth the effort for long-term organizational health.

We May Have Agreed to This. That Doesn't Mean We Follow it

A perfect example of staff not buying in to a strategic plan occurred in a school district where I was an adjunct faculty member helping students find work experience in the community. One of the students, who was barely staying in school, was referred to me by the vice principal. She asked me to treat him as a special case.

I found an employer willing to give him a job on a trial basis. While the student wasn't getting paid, he was earning valuable school credits that could keep him in school. Unfortunately, his work ethic and punctuality were poor and his attitude left a lot to be desired. The employer's leniency had his limits.

I sat in the VP's office telling her that this was the end of the line for the student, and he would have to be accountable for his lack of effort with the employer. If losing his work experience placement meant expulsion from school (he was not producing any effort in other subjects either), then that's how it would have to be.

The VP didn't want to hear that. She wanted me to find him another placement, which I wasn't prepared to do. I didn't think it was in the best interest of the student because the student hadn't earned it, and his behavior had proven he did not value the placement anyway. Losing his placement would be a natural consequence and make him accountable for his behavior.

The VP continued to argue her position, and then I pointed to the wall behind her. There, on her bulletin board in plain view, were the school district's vision statement, mission statement, core values, and guiding principles. I pointed to the guiding principle that read, "*Accountability must be built into every decision.*"

The VP looked at the bulletin board, turned back to me, and said, "Come on, Herky, you're not going to hit me with that crap, are you?" What she meant was, despite all the work the staff in her school division did to come up with value statements, it was just an illusion. They would do what they wanted to do, regardless of what the document said.

It's Much Easier to Score When Everyone Touches the Puck

Strategic plans need to have buy-in from everyone. At the end of the 2014/15 NHL hockey season, the Calgary Flames got eliminated by the Anaheim Ducks in the second round of the Stanley Cup playoffs. The Edmonton Oilers on the other hand, finished the season in 15th place, out of 16 teams, and haven't made the playoffs in 9 years. Why is this important? (Aside from the great pleasure it gives me to needle my Edmonton friends and colleagues!)

About five years prior to the 2014/15 season, the Oilers developed a strategic plan to rebuild their hockey team by drafting skilled young players and avoiding what they called rental players, which are veterans that can help a team do well in the short term. Usually, these players would come to a team on a one or two year contract and then leave.

Because they were doing so poorly in the standings, the Oilers were drafting high and picking some excellent young players. A year or two into the rebuild, there were flashes of brilliance, but still the team wasn't able to compete for a playoff spot. Now, five years into the rebuild, fans are fed up. The Oilers are still at the bottom of the pack, even with all this great young talent.

The Flames, on the other hand, declared their rebuilding strategic plan two years prior to the 2014/15 season. They brought in a new coach and a new general manager, and they too decided to build from the draft or traded for young players. In their second year of the rebuild, the Flames made the playoffs. They have no stars to speak of, compared to the Oilers and have far less raw talent than the Oilers do. What is the difference between these two teams and their relative success during similar rebuilds?

When you listen to Flames coach Bob Hartley speak during the 2014/15 season and playoff run, he raves about how every one of his players bought into the system he and his coaches put in place. The difference between these two organizations is simply buy-in.

The mission statement and strategic plan are the organization's purpose. Everything that is done in the organization should resolve around and reflect that purpose.

When staff truly agree with the mission statement, goals, and desired outcomes, good things happen. The Flames' rebuild and strategic plan has to be considered a great success, at least in comparison to the one implemented by the Oilers. When you have complete buy-in from everyone on staff, the chances of them remembering, believing, and achieving that mission statement increase tremendously.

The mission statement and strategic plan are the organization's purpose. Everything that is done in the organization should revolve around and reflect that purpose. Any policy and procedure manual and decision should be made with this purpose in mind. When that's happening, staff don't need to always consult a policy and procedures manual because they're clear on what the organization is all about. Can you imagine the amount of time this clarity could save in terms of staff time and productivity?

Let's get back to the strategic planning process. If you haven't created a plan yourself, most organizational consultants can facilitate the process, using a model like the one at the beginning of the chapter.

In my opinion, there are two critical mistakes that management make during this process.

I've already mentioned the first, which is ignoring the staff member who may disagree. Strategic planning is not a place for democracy, it's a place for consensus. *Everyone* needs to buy in. Have you ever been in a situation where you were the one person who disagreed with the majority, and you were forced to comply? Could you give 100% to the purpose if you didn't agree with it? Probably not, and your staff will respond similarly if they haven't bought into your organizational purpose and strategic plan. At the very least, those who do not agree with the majority must be heard and some effort needs to be made to understand their concerns and incorporate something about them into the strategic plan.

When You Delegate Responsibility, Let it Go

The second mistake that some management make during a strategic planning process is that they have a pre-conceived vision of the outcome. I've been through sessions where management manipulate, encourage, and coerce to get certain things included in the mission statement or goals and objectives. If you're not prepared to live with whatever your staff comes up with, don't bother going through the process. Just make up your own document, circulate it, and hope that folks adhere to it. (By the way, they won't!). Yes, you can say that it's your company and they should be doing what you ask them to do, but that approach doesn't work for long.

I'm reminded of a one-day team building workshop I facilitated called "Unicorns & Ukuleles." For one of the activities, I brought in a stuffed unicorn that, by the end of the day, as a group we would name. We would then present the newly named unicorn to the CEO.

I informed the CEO of this activity and she said she was fine with it. People submitted their name suggestions on a piece of paper, and we later went through a selection process. All the names were written on a flip chart. The group chose the best five, voted, and eventually picked a winner. The winning name for the unicorn was Dildo Baggins. Yes, you read that right. This was a staff decision and that was the name they chose.

The CEO garnered a lot of respect from me that day because she honored the process. She hated the name, and down the road when I asked how the unicorn was doing, she clearly avoided calling it by that name. The point here is that she was prepared to abide by what her staff wanted. Imagine having gone through the process of naming the unicorn, voting on the winner, and having that vote vetoed by the CEO. This is what happens in many organizations and it's probably the most deflating thing managers can do. If you're not prepared to live with the outcome, don't ask your staff to come up with a plan.

Here are seven tips to make sure your organization has a successful strategic plan:

- Adopt a strategic planning model to create the foundation
- Include all staff in the process of developing the plan
- Make sure all staff have input into the plan
- Make sure every staff buys in to the plan
- Make sure that the plan reflects the purpose of the organization
- Make sure that the plan becomes an integral part of the corporate culture
- Test the impact of the plan on staff by asking them to recite it

Great strategic plans set a course for an organization to be successful. The plan needs to be organic so it can be adapted as circumstances change. Great strategic plans pay huge dividends in helping your organization Get ***F.I.T.,*** and Go Far!

CHAPTER FOUR

Achieve Top ROI Through Professional Development

Your Staff Are Only as Good as the Training They Get

"Investing time to learn something in your profession makes you rich in your knowledge. If you are not, then it will make you poor in your performance."

-Sivaprakash Sidhu

Who Decides What Kind of Training a Professional Should Get?

There is no future for an organization if staff are not continuously growing, learning, and getting better at what they do.

Some organizations are committed to giving their people enough time and money to continue to grow in their jobs, while others toss professional development programs at the first sign of budget cuts. Where does your organization sit on that spectrum?

Are you willing to invest in yourself or your staff? Do you want to run your organization on ideas that worked when the organization was established but are no longer relevant, or do you want to keep up with the times? The choice is yours. We've all seen major corporations die over the last twenty years. The question is, why have they died? My hunch is that a lack of professional development is one of the major reasons.

When I first began teaching, I heard the term professional development (PD) a lot. It seemed to be a huge part of the education system—and remains so today. Teachers have their own conventions every year. The majority of school districts have a PD committee and most schools have a designated PD representative.

Later, when I entered into the business world, I discovered that many organizations were members of associations that had their own conferences. Organizations also seemed to have PD in their budgets to allow staff to get trained in various aspects of their work. Opportunity for PD is out there, and those who take advantage of it stay competitive.

In my first year of teaching, as I was learning the ropes and starving for PD to hone my craft and help me network with other teachers, I remember my very negative first PD experience. The event organizers picked one or two keynote speakers and had a series of breakout sessions. All the teachers in the division came to a central location and spent the day together. It was a mini teachers' convention.

When I read the program I discovered, to my great disappointment, that I wasn't interested in half of what they had planned. To be fair, it's impossible to please every attendee in an event like this. Still, I was frustrated because I was being told how I was going to be developed professionally. I had no freedom to determine what I needed.

The very term "professional" connotes that an individual has some sense of what is needed to grow in their profession. I think it's okay for superiors to make recommendations based on their observations, but to mandate that staff learn something they don't want to learn is a ridiculous notion. I believe my instincts and understanding of my own strengths and limitations should be the driving forces behind what I learn. Forcing me to attend something and calling it "professional development" was an insult to me as a professional, and an indicator that the organization did not trust my professional judgment. That's not the kind of organization I want to work for.

Professional Development should also yield return on investment (ROI). An organization pays money to have their staff trained, and that investment should yield returns. Do you think my school was better off by sending me to a PD day I didn't want to go to? Do you think I was a better teacher after going to that PD day? I don't think so. I was frustrated and resentful, and I doubt if I even remembered which sessions I went to on that day. The return on that investment, if any, was poor.

There are better ways to handle PD. For example, in one school division I worked for, each teacher had his or her own PD budget. It wasn't much, but it was something. And here's the kicker: we got to choose how and where to spend it. This school division recognized that teachers *are* professionals, know themselves better than anyone, and therefore should be able to make their own choices with respect to PD.

We had to run our PD ideas by our administrator, but I think that was really so she knew what was going on and not about getting her permission. It was so refreshing to be able to think about what I wanted and needed to progress as a teacher. I was able to research different topics and attend conferences as I saw fit. I was thrilled to be able to plot my own PD course. If we wanted to attend something that went beyond our allotted PD budget, we could draw on the next year's budget. This organization really understood what PD was all about.

In the scenarios I shared with you, there is no question that it cost more per teacher in the second scenario. It's cheaper to bring every teacher to one central place for a day or two and hope that they get something out of the program, than it is to provide every teacher with their own self-directed PD budget.

If we're talking about ROI though, we must consider intangible yields like improved trust, freedom, attitude, enthusiasm, and self-efficacy. Which scenario do you think had a better ROI based on how this teacher responded? In the first scenario, I became bitter and resentful. That negativity had to have come out in my life and teaching somehow. I'm sure I was not a better teacher when I returned from that first PD experience. In the second scenario, I was excited and ready to return to work, eager to implement the new things I'd learned.

Professional development is a huge part of an organization getting and staying ***F.I.T.*** In fact, PD applies to every aspect of the ***F.I.T.*** acronym. You need to continuously learn to prepare your organization for the future. When your staff is excited, knowledgeable, and empowered, those attributes become part of the corporate culture. Finally, when there is an atmosphere of growth and development, staff work better together as a team, which will ultimately benefits the customer.

Organizations need to adapt quickly, organically, and with purpose. Nothing can help an organization do that more effectively than good professional development. PD is necessary to keep up with fast moving changes in technology. PD can energize staff, and rekindle their desire to be the best they can be. When we stop learning, we start dying.

I hope by now you're getting the impression that I think professional development is a pretty big deal. It shouldn't be just another line in a budget that gets eliminated when things get tough. PD should be at the forefront of every organization, with necessary resources continuously allotted so as to have the best ROI for the organization and the strongest impact on staff.

The Russians Are Not Just Coming, They're Already Here

Through Rotary International, I had the pleasure of leading a vocational exchange team to Russia a number of years ago where I was able to meet and spend time with other organizational consultants. A fellow participant named Stanislav (Stas) Romanenko kindly offered to show me around the city of Krasnodar, which was about the size of Calgary. As we walked the streets, Stas pointed out numerous buildings that housed his clients.

At one point, we entered one of his client's buildings, a sporting goods store, which appeared similar to the Sport Chek stores here in Canada, maybe a little smaller. It was two-stories high, and the layout of the goods was spectacular. Everything looked great, the lighting in the store was excellent, and there was upbeat yet unobtrusive music playing. It gave one the feeling of wanting to spend leisurely time in the store browsing.

There were many young people on staff, all well-groomed, wearing uniforms, smiling, and eager to help. These young employees possessed unusual confidence, and Stas told me why. The owner of this company has sixty of these stores in Russia. Once a young person gets through the interview, he is sent to an intensive training program that appears similar to McDonald's University in North America. There, they spend one month learning about sales, marketing, customer service, and perhaps most importantly, product knowledge.

These kids knew their product and how to do their job well. These Russian youth worked for a base salary and a bonus, yet I saw no sign of competition between them. There was a natural order to things it seemed. They patiently waited, trusting a customer would come along eventually, and they were confident they could make the sale. They didn't try to take customers away from their co-workers.

When Stas and I went upstairs to the second floor of the store, I met the assistant manager. She was twenty-one years old, well groomed, and extremely friendly. She didn't speak English, but as Stas interpreted the conversation for us, I discovered that she had come up through the ranks, having been hired as a high school student, attended the company's training program, and worked her way up to assistant manager in just two years. I asked her what her goal was and, without blinking an eye, she said it was to be a store manager somewhere within the company. I asked her how long she thought it would take for her to do that. She said three to six months.

I was blown away by this experience at a retail store in a country only twenty years out of communist rule. I knew things were changing slowly in the country, and that western ideology was creeping in, but I had not expected this. I asked Stas if his client, the owner of the company, was aware that his professional development training model could make a fortune in North American sporting goods stores. Stas just looked and me, smiled, then said, "He's doing okay right here!"

"US firms spent about $156 billion on employee learning in 2011 ... But with little practical follow-up or meaningful assessments, some 90% of new skills are lost within a year."
-Rachel Silverman

My experience in Russia is a great example of how the right professional development can set an organization apart from its competition. It requires intention on behalf of the organization to make PD a priority. There is no doubt in my mind that the Russian sporting goods store owner was getting a great ROI for training these young people intensively for a month.

The key in the Russian example of PD though is the *right* training. According to Rachel Silverman in the Wall Street Journal in October, 2012, "U.S. firms spent about $156 billion on employee learning in 2011...But with little practical follow-up or meaningful assessments, some 90% of new skills are lost within a year..."

Retention Is the Key to Good Training

Training needs to be well planned and multi-dimensional, and unfortunately that's not always the case. I believe there are three things that organizations *must* do before they send staff to training.

1. Have a clear picture of what their purpose and mission is
2. Clarify what their training objectives are

3. Determine the motivation of the staff who are being trained

Once these issues have been addressed, it's crucial to make sure that the training itself is engaging and incorporates the best methods of learning and retaining information. While the diagram below has created some controversy about how factual it is, or even who was the first to originate it, as a trainer myself, it makes perfect sense to me. I do think we retain information better when we have opportunities to practice and teach others. If these components aren't part of the training events you're sending your staff to, don't expect them to remember much about what they've learned.

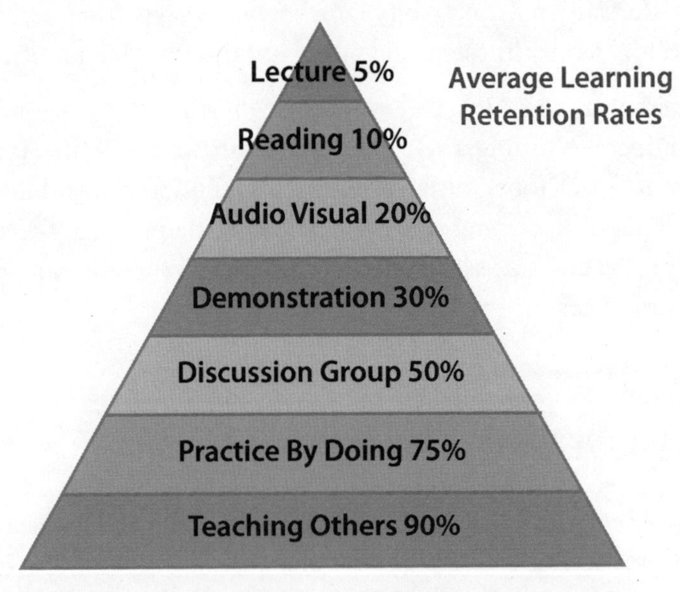

Source: National Training Laboratories, Bethel, Main

Finally, once staff have been trained, there needs to be a plan put in place for implementation of the training back in the workplace.

Here are eight reasons why professional development should be a priority in your organization:

- Better trained employees are more productive.
- PD increases job satisfaction.
- PD increases morale.
- PD motivates employees to do well.
- Well-trained employees adapt to new technologies and procedures faster.
- Lower staff turnover.
- Well-trained employees improve company image.
- It's the right thing to do

We're fortunate in this day and age to be able to take advantage of a wide variety of professional development opportunities. We don't have to restrict ourselves to workshops, conventions, and in-house training.

Here are some other ideas to incorporate into your organization's PD program:

Teams

Setting up teams in your workplace allows for staff to learn from each other on a regular basis through formal team meetings and informal discussion between team members.

Sharing

Set up the opportunity for staff to share what they've learned at off-site conferences with other staff. Teaching what they have learned helps them integrate the material and yields better ROI.

Scenarios

Things happen every day on the job that can be learned from. Why not write up real situations that have happened for staff to discuss and brainstorm how they would deal with them more effectively in the future?

Field Trips

Have staff visit other sites within your organization or other similar organizations where they can conduct interviews and observe how others are doing similar work.

Job Rotation

Give employees the opportunity to try different things in the organization for short periods of time. This provides an excellent understanding of how the total operation works.

In-house Newsletter

Produce a regular publication offering tips and tricks, trends in your industry, and questions for staff to consider that can be discussed at staff meetings.

Job Shadow

Allow staff to shadow other positions within the company that they may want to work in.

Special Projects

Allow for employees to work on a special project that is outside of their normal set of job duties.

Mentoring

Set up an in-house mentoring program where new staff can learn from more experienced workers.

Networking

Set up informal networking opportunities where staff can share ideas and resources with each other.

Performance reviews

Performance reviews can be a great way for staff to learn what they're doing well and what goals they would like to work on.

Feedback

Provide frequent, informal, descriptive feedback to staff on performance.

A great professional development model in your organization can have a huge impact on your people and result in a high

ROI. Don't make the mistake of de-valuing professional development. Prioritize it so your organization can continue to Get ***F.I.T.,*** and Go Far!

CHAPTER FIVE

Preparing Staff to Leave Creates Optimum Performance While They Stay

Grow, Move Up, or Move On

"Being in charge of your work life doesn't mean you always move with assurance and sublime self-confidence; it means you keep moving, continuing on your own path, even when you feel shaky and uncertain."

-Charlotte Beers

Letting Go is the Best Thing You Can Do

Helping your staff plan for their personal futures is a huge part of planning for your organization's future. It will create new leaders in your organization, and open the door for new people to replace those staff whose career path has taken them away from your organization.

Humans have a natural tendency to keep moving. We're driven to search for new, better, and different. Perhaps it stems from our nomadic ancestry, whose survival depended on their ability to move with food sources and the weather. This same tendency occurs in organizations. People want to move. Dave Redekopp, colleague and career development guru in Alberta, Canada refers to this phenomenon as people wanting to *"grow, move up, or move on."* What role then should a manager play in helping her people do that?

While professional development helps your people improve what they do, career development helps them plan for their own future. It could be your most important role as an organizational leader to provide your people the tools and opportunity to grow, move up, or move on. Unfortunately, setting aside resources for career development in organizations is often a lower priority than even professional development. This is a big mistake.

Career development research reveals that in different stages in life, we have different needs with respect to the kind of work we do, the amount of responsibility and leadership we want, and the amount of money we want to earn. Some people are content with doing the same thing at the same level for many years. Most people however, want their careers to progress.

Younger workers today, including those of the millennial generation, have no intention of working toward the gold watch anniversary award. They want to be mobile and they want to work in organizations that recognize that. They also want purpose, goals, and responsibilities, which are all part of a quality career development plan.

What's your organization's career development plan? Is there a clear process for employees to follow which allows and encourages them to move from one point to another? How do you help them become so skilled in their current role that they become mentors for newer staff? Be careful, though. Do not hold these highly skilled employees hostage in their role by withholding opportunities. That's a recipe for disaster, and could lead to those employees leaving the company with bad feelings and resentment.

The career development plan is a systematic approach that outlines how an employee can move from A to B to C and beyond. Goals, objectives, and requirements are laid out so that each employee knows exactly what they have to do to move up. What kind of education and training is required for each of these different levels? What kind of internal support can staff get when applying for these positions, in terms of resume help and preparing them for the next job interview? They may not get the position once they apply for it, but they will at least have developed the necessary skills to be eligible.

Many employers do not want to hear a prospective employee say they have no intention of staying with the organization long-term. To some degree, such reluctance is understandable. Why would an employer invest time, energy, and money, simply to see it walk out the door? But career development is about helping individuals maximize their professional potential. It's about teaching, mentoring, equipping, and preparing them to leave the nest. It's not unlike raising children, investing for their well-being.

Why Parenting is Like Career Development

Parenting is a great metaphor for career development, one that has proven useful countless times over the course of my career. I've worked with at-risk youth for over thirty years in many different capacities. I've been a case worker in residential treatment centers, a group home houseparent, and a youth and family therapist. I've also designed parenting programs and have facilitated numerous training programs for parents. Am I an expert at parenting? Absolutely not. But I will stake my reputation on the following advice.

I believe your job as a parent is to help your kids become as self-sufficient as possible, so they can be well-equipped to move into the world with confidence and assurance. Without even realizing it, that's exactly what my parents did with me. I don't think they were conscious of this parenting trick at all. I think I was just on my own so much that I learned to take care of myself. Consequently, I was out the door right after I finished high school at age seventeen.

Your job as an organizational leader is to help your employees become as self-sufficient as possible – so much so, that they might decide to leave your organization.

Similarly, I believe your job as an organizational leader is to help your employees become as self-sufficient as possible - so much so, that they might decide to leave your organization. There's a bit of a paradox here; the more encouragement you give your employees to spread their wings and fly, the more apt they may be to actually stay with you. After all, it's tough to leave a place that cares so much about you. (Any of your kids returning to the nest?)

The time and care you invest pays off. Eventually, you can see the fruits of your labor as your children grow into caring human beings with positive self-esteem who reach out to help others. This ripple effect has the potential to change the world in significant ways.

When studies are done on organizational wellness, leadership style is always one of the factors in examining how employees feel about the workplace. One of the outcomes of conflict between staff and management is an increased level of absenteeism. The Conference Board of Canada published a study in 2013 called *"Missing in Action: Absenteeism Trends in Canadian Organizations"* and they estimated that the direct cost of absenteeism to the Canadian economy was $16.6 billion in 2012.

In organizations where employees feel uncared for, it's reasonable to assume that there may be a higher degree of absenteeism that is costly in terms of productivity, morale, and ultimately the bottom line. Paying attention to an employee's career development is a great way to show you care.

If career development is about developing individuals, that in itself might put some employers off because they feel that the needs of individuals should come second to those of the organization. But the two are not mutually exclusive. An organization is comprised of individuals. If what's best for the organization is not best for the individuals within, then it may not be best at all.

In my own organization when I employed staff, both paid and volunteer, there was no question that when the individuals in my company felt happy and taken care of, we progressed effectively. Sometimes, it meant spending a lot more time on someone's personal issues for example, but in the long run, it was time well spent. I also always encouraged my staff to feel free to work somewhere else if that's what they wanted. No guilt necessary. Then the paradox mentioned earlier kicks in. I rarely lost anybody unless a contract ended. When you treat people right, they tend to want to stay.

The number one reason employees are satisfied with their jobs is because they enjoy their work. We managers need to make sure that our staff enjoy what they do. If they don't, we need to make adjustments. That's why professional development and career development are critical to helping organizations Get ***F.I.T.***

As a youth and family therapist, I met many parents who did not want their kids to be independent or self-sufficient. They *said* they did, but their behavior communicated something different. Those types of parents were often controlling, co-dependent, or living vicariously through their kids. We've all known people like that, and have witnessed the results of that type of parenting. In fact, they're probably working in your organization right now. You've likely got the whole spectrum of employees, from self-sufficient and independent, to controlling and co-dependent.

Don't you think your job then, as managers and supervisors, is to spend whatever time and energy is necessary to help the people who work for you to become better people, both personally and professionally? You may not see the fruits of your labor immediately, or ever for that matter. But ultimately, you are providing a service to the world, and I believe that generosity of spirit will be returned to you many times over in some way.

What's good for the company may or may not be good for the individual, and what's good for the individual may or may not be good for the company. What's good for the individual though, in terms of helping them to become the best they can be, always makes the world a better place.

When I first became a teacher, the path to becoming a team leader, school administrator, or a manager at the district level was clearly mapped out. There was comfort in that, whether or not I had the ambition to move up. I knew that if I wanted to, I could. And I knew what I had to do in order to make it happen.

What do you have in place to show your employees exactly what they have to do in order to move up the ladder? What's your career development plan? Have you asked your people where they want to be in five years? And, have you given them permission to say, "*Out of here?*"

What Do You Want to Be When You Grow Up?

One of the most important things I've learned through my career development experience is the importance of transferable skills. When I finally understood this concept, it really helped me in my work with youth, and then with adults later on.

I would ask a classroom full of students, for example, what profession they aspired to, and used someone's answer as the focus of our discussion. Let's say a student said they wanted to be a veterinarian. I wrote that up on the board. Then I'd suggest that the students consider a fast food job at McDonald's. I'd ask them - even if they hated thinking about working there - what skills they thought they needed to be the best McDonald's worker ever. They suggested skills like being good with money, people skills, working well under pressure, and being punctual.

I would compile this huge list of skills and attributes on the board and ask, "Is there anything on this list that you wouldn't need to be a great veterinarian?" The answer would almost always be no. This is a great exercise to help people understand there are many skills that are transferable from one job to another.

Of course, for either job, working at McDonald's or being a vet, there are skills that one can only learn from school or on the job experience. This is what I refer to as the *science* of work. How the job is performed though, is the *art* of work, and where transferable skills are most applicable.

Using the answers from your employees as to where they see themselves in five years, we can apply the same principle as I did with those students. You can help your people see that much of what they're doing and learning in your organization is transferable to where they want to be in the future. They may realize then, that they might not be in such a hurry to move on.

Changed Lives, Changed Organizations

"Career development changes organizations by helping them to become stronger, more innovative, and to become employers of choice."
-Paula Wischoff-Yerama

There's another reason for helping your people develop their career paths and perhaps ultimately leave your company for additional challenges in their professional lives. I'll borrow a story from my friend Les Kletke, because it illustrates this point so well. His friend John was a minor league baseball manager, whose team was in a very small, out-of-the-way market that not a whole lot of people would have died to be a part of. A young kid approached John for permission to do the play-by-play for the team on the radio. John thought the kid had some personality, some baseball knowledge, and was teachable in terms of what an announcer would need to know, so he gave him the job.

Given where the team was located, the boy's chances at advancing in the broadcasting career were slim. With John's help and advice as to how to become a better broadcaster, the kid moved on. Around eight years later, John received a phone call from the kid, who was fully grown by that time. He invited John to a Minnesota Twins game as a thank you for helping him become a TSN broadcaster.

What a gift to be able to give someone your experience, support, and encouragement so they can fly on their own to places yet unknown. Career development within organizations is not just a feel-good thing. It changes lives. And, as my friend and career development specialist, Paula Wischoff-Yerama says, career development "...also changes organizations by helping them to become stronger, more innovative, and to become employers of choice."

To recap, how do you help your employees grow, move up, or move on? Here are eight steps you can take toward implementing a career development program in your organization to help it Get ***F.I.T.,*** and Go Far!

- Define career development for your organization.
- Determine what materials and resources you may need.
- Hire consultants or use your HR department.
- Set goals and objectives.
- Make sure to get employee buy-in.
- Have each employee develop a career plan including future aspirations, skill gaps, professional development needs, and timeframe.
- Pilot the program.
- Evaluate and modify.

IDENTITY

"Our emerging workforce is not interested in command-and-control leadership. They don't want to do things because I said so; they want to do things because they want to do them."

-Irene Rosenfeld

How the organization is perceived by others, including employees, competitors, and customers

CHAPTER SIX

Create Harmony Through Managing Multi-Generations in the Workplace

Where You Come from Matters

"Each generation imagines itself to be more intelligent than the one that went before it, and wiser than the one that comes after it."

-George Orwell

Talkin' About My G-Generation -Pete Townshend

When speaking about an organization's identity, one important factor to consider is the makeup of the workforce within that organization.

For the first time in history, there are five generations of workers in the workplace; The Matures, the Baby Boomers, Generation X, Generation Y (Millennials), and now Generation Z. Each person from each generation brings a unique perspective on the world of work. Those perspectives are developed through individual experiences, influences, and filters.

The result is a complex web of differing values, work performance, and approaches to interactions with others at work. In my experience as an organizational consultant, this web can create monumental challenges for management.

Do you have any generational issues in your workplace? Are there members of an older generation, for example, who dismiss members of a younger generation for one reason or another? It could be their hair color, piercings, or tattoos, the way they talk, their perceived work ethic, or a myriad of other reasons. Do you have young workers who have no patience for older workers and think they do things the "old fashioned" way?

How do you manage this array of personalities, values, and experience? What do you need to know to bridge the generational gap? How can you make every employee, regardless of generation, feel a part of the team?

A number of years ago, I was fortunate enough to create a project that answered these questions. Having worked with youth and employers for much of my adult life, I was aware of the issues both employers and employees faced in the workplace. The idea was to get a number of organizations involved, gather some information on whether or not they felt they had any issues in their workplace due to generational differences, see if I could find some common ground, then facilitate a one-day training event to share issues, educate folks on generational differences, and provide some ways to bridge the generation gap.

The first part was easy. I found six organizations willing to participate: a rural car dealership, an urban car dealership, two grocery chain stores, a rural bank, and a rural town recreation complex. I wanted a relatively small sample due to budget constraints, but at the same time to have enough information to identify generational issues that were consistent from organization to organization.

The second piece of the project was no surprise based on my research and personal experience. I gathered information from an anonymous survey and then facilitated some focus groups which dug a little deeper into the survey responses. Each organization had its share of generational issues, and five out of the six wanted to go to the next level which was to participate in a customized training day. The rural car dealership opted out.

The issues spanned a wide spectrum of workplace activity. To summarize the results in one statement: older generations looked down on younger generations for all kinds of reasons, and younger generations didn't think their elders should be so critical of them.

The result wasn't surprising except for one part. Of the ten questions I posed to employees, one answer in particular shocked me. I asked the participants to rate various things that were important to them at work, including pay, opportunity for advancement, using their skills and abilities on the job, learning new things, and having a say in how the company was run.

R-E-S-P-E-C-T...Find Out What it Means to Me -Otis Redding

A whopping 69% of the participants from across all the generations chose "being treated with more respect" as the most important thing to them in the workplace. The second most important thing to them, with 46% weighing in, was having "the opportunity to use your skills and talents to the maximum." In case you're wondering, "salary" tied for fourth place at 41%.

69% of the participants from across all the generations chose, "being treated with more respect" as the most important thing to them in the workplace.

To me, the results of this survey were significant. I found the common thread that could be woven throughout an organization, regardless of how big or small, and how many generations of workers it employed. A lot of the other issues in organizations matter less to most of us, but show us some respect for who we are and what we can offer, and we would go to war for you.

This notion of respect pops up frequently. Have you ever looked at a young person who has orange hair, piercings, tattoos and ragged clothes, and started to make some judgments about who he is, what he might value, and whether or not he would be good for your company? On the other hand, have you ever done the same thing to someone who is well dressed, well-coiffed, and well spoken? I don't think I have to tell you that history is filled with stories of those who fit the latter description and have done some terrible things in society.

When we judge people, our respect for an individual is biased by that judgment. If the judgment is good, we respect them. If the judgment is bad, we may not. That judgment, often formulated from a quick first impression, can last a lifetime. When was the last time you were judged in a way that contradicted what you believed about yourself? How did that feel?

In the workplace, if one doesn't feel respected by management and co-workers, it will have an impact on his production. I don't know about you, but when I feel respected, cared for, appreciated, and wanted in the place I'm working, I work a lot harder, and with more commitment to my job. In some places where the economy does well, organizations are finding out just how quickly their employees will migrate to another workplace if they don't feel respected, regardless of the salary and opportunity.

With the information I gathered from surveys and focus groups, I was ready to develop the one-day training program for the remaining five organizations. I had identified the common thread of respect, and found a way to get the participants to understand the importance of respect and how we can change our perspective of others.

One element of the training agenda was to provide some information on the differences between each generation. Most participants weren't aware of some of these powerful influences on our behavior. For example, can we really blame Generation Y youth for coming across sometimes as feeling they are entitled to things? After all, where did they learn this? Perhaps it was modelled by the parent who said, "I've worked hard all week and now I'm entitled to a relaxing weekend," or, "I've worked hard all year so now I'm entitled to a four week vacation." What about, "I live in Canada so I'm entitled to medical insurance," or "I've worked hard all my life so now I'm entitled to a government pension."

I don't think Generation Y kids are born with this sense of entitlement. I think they learn it from us. When I brought these issues up at the training session, it was an eye-opener for many. If we understand a person's story, where they came from, and what they have gone through in their lives, we are more apt to understand that person's behavior, and more able to accept and ultimately respect them.

Stereotyping Can Be Dangerous

I presented an activity at the training session based on my work *Using Music as a Career Development Tool*. This activity helps create awareness about stereotyping. I use music because music is universal and breaks down barriers between people. One need only attend a folk festival for example, to see people of all ages and colors enjoying the music together yet in individual ways. In my experience working with young people, I find music engages humans in one of the most powerful ways possible.

For the training activity, I placed a number of posters on the wall around the room. Each poster listed two or three musical genres that related to each other in some way. For example, "Rock/Blues," "Opera/Classical," or "Punk/Alternative/Metal." I then asked the participants to review the posters and stand next to the one that spoke most directly to them at that moment. Once everyone gathered under a particular poster, I instructed participants to note who was standing where. Do you think they started to make judgments about people based on where they were standing? Of course they did.

A classic example occurred when I conducted this activity with a school's staff, and the only person standing under the "Punk/ Alternative" poster was the principal - the Mormon principal. At first, the staff thought he was joking, but it turned out he wasn't, and he challenged them to check out his MP3 player to see what was on it.

After some discussion, I asked the staff members if their collective impression of this principal had changed because of the kind of music he liked, and perhaps more importantly, did they have a particular impression about him as a clean-cut Mormon principal prior to this activity? Can you see how some stereotypes could be developed about him based on who he was, and now, on his choice of music?

The next step in this activity was to brainstorm with other participants standing in their group about common characteristics of people who listen to their kind of music. The results were telling. Usually, if you believe something is good (punk music, for example) you speak positively about the music and the people who listen to it. So, characteristics like rebellious, risk-taker, and high energy might come up in a group who likes punk music. Can you think of any other musical genres where these characteristics might also be suggested? Risk-taker for rock music perhaps? Rebellious for folk music?

As we go through this process, the participants begin to realize that we all have many similarities, preferences, and even character defects, but just because we listen to a certain kind of music, doesn't make us right, wrong, or better. Can the same be said for people who have tattoos or piercings, dye their hair orange, wear loafers, or eat watermelon for breakfast?

If we're going to judge people for anything in the workplace, it should be for their character, work ethic, how they treat and work with others, and how they help the organization achieve a common goal. It's really about finding common ground with others. When we do that, we appreciate what each one brings to the workplace in terms of skill, experience, personality, and potential.

Everyone Brings Something to the Table

The last activity in the training program was a simulated event to increase sales in each organization. I divided up the teams according to their generations. What do you think happened?

Each generation brought back solid ideas for the best way to run a sales event and attract customers. They did it differently, but everyone could see the merit in each proposal, and understood it made no difference that the group presenting their plan preferred punk, jazz, or folk music. It was all about the goal of increasing sales and attracting customers.

Is there a generation gap in your workplace? Each generation's experience might be different than the other, but the emotional contexts are all the same. Each generation has experienced fear, anger, frustration, joy, happiness, and love. That's our common ground.

The key to managing a multi-generational workplace is to find common ground, learn about each other, appreciate the skills, experience, personality, and potential of each individual, and foster an organizational culture of respect. If you as a manager are willing to do that, your organization will indeed Get ***F.I.T.,*** and Go Far!

Here are six things you can do to address multi-generations in your organization:

- Have a professional development day that includes educating your staff on each of the generations.
- Create an anonymous survey and ask your staff if they think there are any generational issues in your workplace.
- Consider engaging external consultants or speakers who specialize in multi-generational issues in the workplace to conduct workshops or training with your employees.

- Create a simulated problem relevant to your organization and have employees work in teams to solve it. If your organization is big enough, the teams can be composed of employees who are all in the same generation. If your organization is smaller, each team can include a member from each generation.
- Encourage an open dialogue amongst your staff members about differences between them, and how the organization can use those differences to their advantage.
- If respect is an important quality in your organization, ask your employees how they would like to be shown more respect by management or their co-workers.

CHAPTER SEVEN

Use "Power With" Leadership to Produce Results

You May Be the Leader, But is Anybody Following?

"If your actions inspire others to dream more, learn more, do more and become more, you are a leader."

-John Quincy Adams

What Type of Leader Are You?

There is no question that leadership makes or breaks an organization, and that the leader is a huge part of an organization's identity. I've seen organizations that can't move forward in a productive way despite having fantastic staff, because of poor leadership.

What makes a good leader? In my opinion, leaders set the tone, provide the motivation, and define the culture of the organization. Good leaders inspire their staff to be great. They teach and facilitate learning. Good leaders are role models for their staff, and know when to get out of the way.

In Chapter Fifteen, I will ask you to determine what kind of a decision maker you are: democratic, autocratic, consensus, or collective. In this chapter, I'm going to ask what you think your leadership style is. If you like, you can use the four categories of decision making to determine your leadership style. There are also many short leadership quizzes and assessments you can take online if you search for "leadership style."

Daniel Goleman's work, *Leadership That Gets Results* outlines six leadership styles, and may help you determine your own style. Below is a brief overview of each type.

The pacesetting leader

This type of leader can be thought of as saying "*Do as I do...now!*"

The authoritative leader

Helps the team work toward a common vision and is a "Come with me" type of leader.

The affiliative leader

This is the leader that believes "People come first" and works to create emotional bonds within an organization. This leader is the nurturer.

The coaching leader

This leader builds for the future by helping staff develop their personal strengths, and can be thought of as saying, "*Try this.*"

> *The "my way or the highway" style of leadership is going the way of the dinosaur. We are seeing more "power with" or "leading from behind" leadership styles that will move organizations forward.*

The coercive leader

This is the "Do what I tell you" type of leader.

The democratic leader

This leader helps to build consensus through participation. This leader can be thought to say, "*What do you think?*"

You may find that your leadership style encompasses more than one of these styles, and indeed, there are moments within an organization's lifespan when some leadership styles work better than others. It's always good to assess where one stands in this area, but it's also a good idea to ask your staff what they think about you in terms of your leadership style. Get them to complete one of the leadership assessments, but sit down while you read it. It may not be what you expected.

"My Way or the Highway" Just Doesn't Cut it Anymore

In my master's thesis, I explored the concept of "power with" as opposed to "power over" leadership. "Power with" leadership combines the traits of the pacesetter, the affiliate, the coach, and the democrat. It is truly about making decisions together as a team, and even though the leader is ultimately responsible for any decisions made, they are made with staff.

"Power with" leadership requires a willingness to give up power, and for some that is a very difficult thing to do. Another way to look at this type of leadership is "leading from behind." In Linda Hill's blog on Leading From Behind, she quotes Nelson Mandela, who, in his autobiography, compared leadership to being a shepherd. He said of the shepherd, *"He stays behind the flock, letting the most nimble go out ahead, whereupon the others follow, not realizing that all along they are being directed from behind."*

The world is rapidly changing, and global competition and innovation are at the forefront of how an organization goes about its business. Add to that the changing nature of the worker. People want work that is meaningful, and to have input into how it gets done. Traditional leadership styles don't work anymore in this environment. The "my way or the highway" style of leadership is going the way of the dinosaur. We are seeing more "power with" or "leading from behind" leadership styles that will move organizations forward.

I was fortunate enough to experience a wonderful example of this "power with" leadership style during my tenure as a guidance counsellor at the Alternative High School. The school had been around for quite some time, was one of the schools within the Calgary Board of Education, and held special status. It was capped at 120 students, who could not, or would not succeed in the other "regular" schools in the system. It might be considered a type of charter school in today's North American educational system.

This school was founded based on the tenets of any democratic organization. All school-related issues that were not school board policy were handled in a democratic fashion through weekly "town meetings." Students were taught to run these meetings through their social studies class, and anyone in the school could add items to the weekly agenda. With only twelve staff and 120 students, it was possible that the students could out-vote the staff on every issue, and literally run the school. To some extent they did, and that was the very thing that allowed many of these students to achieve the success in school that they never had before.

How can this work? How can a school be successful with such a system in place, where students held much of the power? The leadership style of its principal made it possible. Without really knowing it, he was practicing "power with" or "leading from behind" leadership. In staff meetings, we used a consensus decision making model, and if that couldn't work, it was at least democratic in nature. In every case, the principal, who was ultimately responsible for anything we did at the school, was willing to relinquish his power and abide by the choices of the students and staff.

The results of this type of leadership were extraordinary. As a staff member, I could be exactly who I was, speak up for or against an issue without fear of retribution. It was not staff versus students. It was a group of people who were encouraged to debate issues, influence each other through their passion and their knowledge about issues, and accept the decisions made by the group.

Now-famous pop star, Leslie Feist, is an Alternative High School graduate. The day after she won five Juno music awards at the ceremonies in Calgary in 2008, she visited her Alma Mater. It must have been a very special place for her to do that after all those years, and so soon after her major accomplishment.

From a student perspective, they had never experienced this kind of power before, and it changed many of their lives. The regular school system suppressed their individuality and tried to make them conform to a system that they had virtually no impact upon. At Alternative High, they *were* the school. It was their ideas, their artwork, and their vision that drove the school. At Alternative High, there were very few instances of bullying, theft, or vandalism. It represented the possibilities inherent in this model of shared governance.

This school was indeed an anomaly in the educational world, and in the organizational world as well. Our leader truly encompassed "power with" leadership. He was an excellent example of the kind of leader President Teddy Roosevelt spoke about when he coined the phrase, "*Speak softly and carry a big stick; you will go far.*"

The principal at Alternative High had the "big stick" inherent in his position as principal, but he rarely used it. Instead, he walked softly allowing and encouraging others to emerge as leaders and share the responsibility of making decisions that were in the best interest of the majority. This experience for many of us, students and staff alike, made a world of difference in terms of our desire to be a part of this place. Staff loved coming to work and students loved attending school - the same students that had hated school, and were deemed to be unsuccessful in the regular system.

Another example of an innovative idea was when the school backed one of its students to run for city council based on a number of environmental issues that the students felt were lacking in the city. While the student didn't win a seat on council, she received over ten thousand votes. Not bad for a high school student.

Being Different from You is a Good Thing

Alternative High leadership illustrates the power of encouragement and validating different points of view within an organization. People with different points of view often get overlooked. Is the same thing going on in your organization? Are you training and promoting people who will maintain the status quo? If you are, then you may have a problem.

The Alternative High example shows us that we can allow for differences of opinion — differences that give the school life and character and move the school forward. What moves your organization forward?

Is your staff inspired in your organization? If not, I can guarantee your customers won't be inspired either. What can you do within your organization to inspire others? I think the very first thing you can do is determine *why* you do *what* you do. Simon Sinek's book *Start With Why* is a great place to look if you haven't thought about this question. Many of us know what we do, but surprisingly few can articulate why we do it. I talk more about Sinek's work in Chapter Nine.

Once you determine the why for what you do, assess your own leadership style. Then get all the other managers and supervisors in your organization to do the same. I encourage you to have your staff evaluate your leadership style to see if those results are the same as your own self-assessment.

I would also urge you to consider the leaders within your organization and encourage staff who have very different ideas than your own to become leaders themselves. We need to set aside our fear of having people with different ideas take charge. In doing so, the organization has the opportunity to flourish in new and innovative ways.

Leaders are the key to organizations, and leadership style can make or break your organization. Determine what yours is, and make changes if necessary so that your organization can Get ***F.I.T.,*** and Go Far!

CHAPTER EIGHT

Establish a Unique Corporate Culture and Increase Customer Loyalty

Branding Doesn't Work with Just Cattle

"The thing I have learned at IBM is that culture is everything."

-Louis V. Gerstner Jr.

I'd Like to Teach the World to Sing

Corporate culture is a major part of an organization's identity, and has been defined as "a blend of the values, beliefs, taboos, symbols, rituals, and myths all companies develop over time."

If you can accept this as a working definition, then how would you describe your corporate culture? What are your values and beliefs? What topics are taboo in your organization? What symbols represent your corporate brand? What rituals or ceremonies perpetuate this corporate culture, and what are the myths that have lingered in your organization over time?

If you can't answer at least several of these questions, then you may not have a true corporate culture. More importantly, if there are only a few people within the organization that can answer them, you still don't have a corporate culture. You may be asking, "So what? Why is corporate culture important?"

Corporate culture is important because it *defines* the organization. It's the brand of the organization, if you will. When we think about an organization's culture, an image comes to mind. For example, what would you say the culture of Apple is? Is it just a company that sells electronics or is it something more? When I think of Apple, I also think of words like rebellious, cutting edge, and innovative.

What about Coca Cola? Is it just another company that produces soft drinks? When I think of Coke, I think about much more than just a soft drink. I think of their classic commercial jingle from decades ago: "*I'd like to teach the world to sing in perfect harmony,*" with people of all ages and colors singing together, or the Super Bowl commercial with people from all over the world singing *America the Beautiful.*

Coca Cola is trying to sell us something more than soft drinks. They're trying to sell us the notion that we can bring the world together (with a soft drink? perhaps!), that people of all races and colors can get along, be together, sing together, and change the world. I don't feel any of that when I drink a Pepsi.

How about Walt Disney Studios? What do you think of when you think of Disneyland? Theme parks? Movies? Animation? I think of all of those things too, but above all, I think of Disney as an organization that brings families together through fun, entertainment, and creativity. There is an amusement park in my home city of Montreal called Belmont Park. It didn't embody my perceptions of Disneyland, however. I think about Belmont Park as a place to go for a bit of leisure time, period.

If an organization has an identity like those mentioned, and we associate it with things that are meaningful in life, like innovation, family, and bringing people together, it will be more successful in the long run. Therefore, developing a corporate culture is highly important. It speaks to why we do the things we do, not just the what or how.

Walk the Talk

It's important to point out that many organizations mislead consumers, maybe not intentionally, but it happens. They tell us they stand for something (culture), which attracts us to buy their goods or services. However, we eventually find out that what goes on behind the marketing does not always match the image they portray. (Will buying Budweiser really get me beautiful women, great friends, and an active lifestyle?)

I was misled this way when applying to be a corporate trainer with a large construction company. After doing a tremendous amount of research on the company, I was struck by the image it portrayed online. That image was one of a solid, straightforward company that has become huge because of innovation, risk-taking, and out-of-the-box thinking. This was a corporate culture I wanted to be a part of.

Having made it through the initial phone interview, I was asked to come to corporate headquarters and do a thirty-minute presentation to the training team. The topic for the exercise could be anything, and the purpose of the presentation was for the training team to evaluate my presentation skills, and how well I engaged the audience.

As a trainer, I have many topics I could present on, but because of what I read about the company, I wanted to do something unique for them. When I got to corporate headquarters, I was excited. And I was even more ecstatic when I saw that one entire wall was covered with a giant word cloud, filled with all the powerful words I'd seen online that defined the company's culture. I felt I was in the right place and anticipated great things.

The presentation began with me explaining the scenario, then taking the group through a series of relevant, interactive, and fun activities. The group was highly engaged. They were laughing. They were listening. They were participating. I was feeling damn good about myself and the choice I made to do something unique.

After the presentation, I waited forty-five minutes for the group to decide my fate, and then I was called into an office with three members of the team. While they felt my presentation was fun and engaging, they said it lacked substance and wasn't what they wanted to see. They wanted a more traditional training style with the trainer speaking and the participants listening. I didn't get the job.

I have to tell you that my pride was hurt and I left the building disappointed. Did I miss something in my research? Did the company give me a false impression of who they were? Didn't they want innovative, out-of-the box thinkers? It appeared that they actually wanted traditional trainers, and I was anything but.

To me, this is an example of a company not walking that talk. I will repeat however that this is a huge construction company, so they must be doing something right. It's just that their branding seemed to conflict with the reality of their organizational culture.

Change Your Culture and You Can Change the World

On the other side of the coin, an organization's culture can also be shifted to change people's perceptions about that organization. After completing my education degree, I was hired to be the new teacher in an alternative education program in rural British Columbia.

When I got to the school, I was introduced to the reputation (culture) of the program. The program had its own portable classroom, separated from the main school building, and the students who attended the program were known as troublemakers, losers, and dummies. This description of the students was not only coming from other students, it also came from teachers and adults in the community. The program had been running for about five years and there wasn't one student from it who graduated high school.

Without knowing I was doing so at the time, I set about changing the culture of the program. I asked the students if they knew what their reputation was. They pretty much did. Then I asked if they wanted to do something about it, and they asked how. During that first year, we rarely did any academic work. What we did was build self-esteem. We also cleaned up the portable to make it look great, and renamed the program, "The Back Door Program." We then generated ideas as to how we could change the culture.

We came up with lots of ideas, and they all revolved around helping improve the school, the community, and the world at large. We cleaned up around the school, and developed a business in the community gathering empty bottles, doing yard work, and shoveling snow. With the money we raised, we adopted third world children and placed their pictures and bios in the school display cases with our name on them. Things shifted...slowly...but they shifted.

The Back Door Program came to be known as a group of students with some academic and social challenges who really cared about each other, their school, their community, and the world. They showed this through their actions. As the students felt better about themselves, the academic wheels eventually kicked in and after three years we had about an 80% graduation rate.

Culture defines the purpose of the organization. Once everyone in the organization knows the purpose, everything they do should reflect that purpose.

The culture of the Back Door Program changed so dramatically that students from the regular school wanted to know how get into the program. Teachers wanted to come visit the portable, something they had never done before, to see what was going on. Is culture important? Absolutely.

The construction company and the Back Door Program are two examples of how corporate culture works. The first illustrates a culture inside an organization that says one thing and does another. The second, a program that had a negative culture, demonstrates that people can make a conscious decision to change that culture. Their walk matched their talk. They became attractive to others who also wanted self-esteem, success, pride, and purpose.

That really is what corporate culture is all about isn't it? It defines the purpose of the organization. Once everyone in the organization knows the purpose, everything they do should reflect that purpose.

These changes to the culture had profound impacts on everyone at the school. Students were engaged, parents and teachers were surprised, and the community and school benefited from the new behavior that resulted. Students graduated from high school, other students wanted to get into the program, teachers were curious and even envious of the program's attention. Small changes over time created a huge impact.

What would these kinds of changes mean to your organization? What would they do to impact the attitude of your employees? How would changes in attitude affect productivity and customer service? Establishing a corporate culture that is meaningful, relevant, and definable is an important part of organizations getting ***F.I.T.***

Courageous Organizational Development

How can you go about doing this? I use a tool called the Circle of Courage© to help organizations begin this process. The Circle of Courage is a concept developed by North American Aboriginals, and used in a program developed by Larry Brendtro and Martin Brokenleg to help at-risk youth.

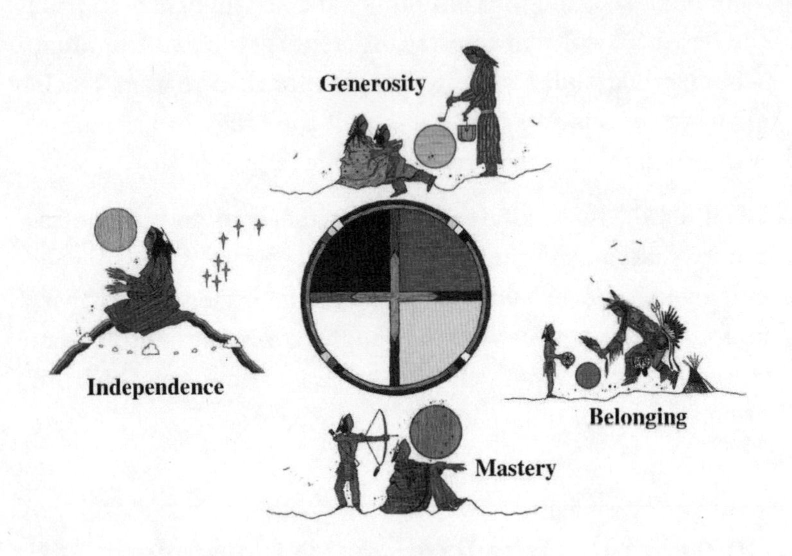

The Circle of Courage from Reclaiming Youth International

The Circle of Courage© model features four distinct components; generosity, belonging, mastery, and independence. What I do with organizations is have employees work on the opportunities they have within their organization to demonstrate each of the four components. What we get at the end of this exercise is an excellent visual of all the things the organization does well in terms of helping employees become better at what they do (mastery), providing volunteer opportunities for employees (generosity), showing employees they are cared for in the organization (belonging), and helping employees become better leaders and decision-makers within the organization (independence).

The results reflect true corporate culture, regardless of what they say they stand for. This work with the Circle of Courage© will determine whether or not organizations are walking their talk. If they're not, the second exercise is an opportunity for the organization to change. Part two is brainstorming all the possible things an organization can do to improve the opportunities in each component of the circle.

Once all the possibilities are generated, I take the group through a process to prioritize, create an action plan, and implement the plan. If an organization is willing to do this, they will align their actions with their words, and everyone in the organization will be on board.

This exercise is a way to determine corporate culture, or to get it back on track. The energy shifts in an organization that goes through this process with the intention of getting better. Staff feel heard, empowered, and appreciated. Management are excited that their employees are working together and are committed to change the corporate culture. People are happy in their work. As you can imagine, increased productivity and better customer service soon follow.

In organizations that have an observable and defined culture, people can *feel* the positive energy when they walk in the building, and when they meet the staff. People want to work there. People want to buy their products and be a part of the experience.

When You Wish Upon a Star

Did you know that at Walt Disney theme parks, if you ask an employee a question that they can't answer, they will take you by the hand and find someone else on staff who can before they leave you? How many other organizations do you know that will do that? Think of the times you've been on the phone trying to make a complaint about something, and how many people you have to go through, telling the same story over and over before you ever, *if* you ever, get any satisfaction.

You may also be aware that Disney sells customer service programs and trains people all over the world in these techniques. There is a reason for their huge, long term success. It's a corporate culture that people identify with, it's products and services that are attractive to people, and it's all backed by superior customer service.

If your organization doesn't have a defined corporate culture, then I strongly urge you to start developing one, or begin reworking the one you have. Start by answering the following questions discussed earlier in the chapter:

What are your corporate values and beliefs?
What are the things that are taboo in your organization?
What symbols represent your corporate brand?
What rituals or ceremonies do you have that perpetuate this corporate culture?
What are the myths that have lingered
in your organization over time?

Corporate culture is a major part in helping organizations Get ***F.I.T.,*** and Go Far!

CHAPTER NINE

Unlock the Why, Speak from the Inside Out, and Increase Your Bottom Line

The Golden Circle

"People don't buy what you do, they buy why you do it."

-Simon Sinek

Everyone Wants to Know Why

People identify strongly with organizations that are able to articulate why they do the things they do.

What is the purpose of your organization? Why do you do what you do? When decisions are made in your organization, are they based on what it is you do in your organization, or the "why"? What about your employees? How do they make decisions? Are they sifting through policies and procedures manuals for clues, or making decisions based on their understanding of the corporate purpose?

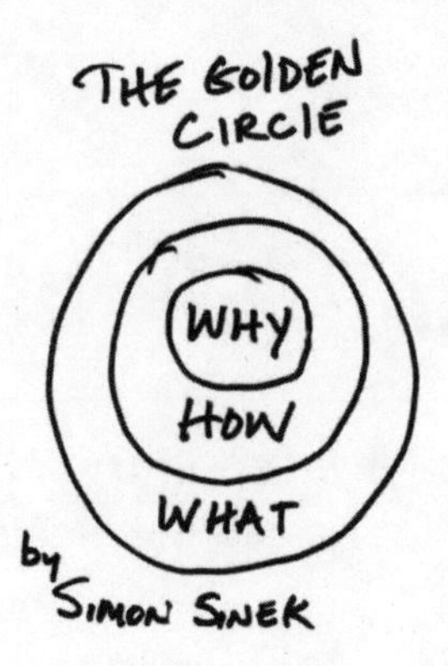

The importance of "why" can't be understated. While writing this book, I read *Start With Why* by Simon Sinek, and I have to say, it changed my life. Sinek explains his theory of the Golden Circle, made of three concentric circles with "why" in the innermost circle, "how" in the middle circle, and "what" in the outer circle. He explains how organizations usually communicate from the outside in. That is, many organizations can tell you what they do, and most can also tell you how they do it, but many can't tell you why they do what they do.

The "why" is the purpose of the organization. In my experience, even if the CEO or senior management can tell you the why few employees can. Go ahead, take this challenge. Ask your employees, *"Why do we do what we do?"* I think you'll be surprised by the answers.

Instead of communicating from the outside in, Sinek suggests that organizations should communicate from the inside out. This means that first we have to know our "why." Once we know the purpose of our organization, everything else should fall into place. Decisions can be based on how their outcomes relate to "why." Outcomes are results, or the "what" in Sinek's Golden Circle theory.

Imagine if all of your employees knew the why of your organization; they would be empowered by knowing the purpose of the organization. If employees know this, and are inspired by it, it makes it easier for them to make decisions and ultimately provide great customer service.

> *"75-85% of start-up businesses fail within the first 3-5 years primarily because the why was not supported with the how and what."*
> *-Wayne Mann*

If your employees know the why, they don't always have to run to managers to ask questions to make decisions. Not every single little thing needs to be written down in a four-inch thick policies and procedures manual. Knowing the why lessens the load on senior management and gives more responsibility to employees, which will help them develop their leadership skills so they can eventually move into management positions.

Don't get me wrong. While knowing the why is fundamentally important for an organization, it means nothing without also knowing "what" the organization does in terms of the goods and services it provides, the desired outcomes for consumers who purchase those goods and services, and "how" they go about delivering those goods and services.

Wayne Mann, business coach and friend, states it well: *"75-85% of start-up businesses fail within the first 3-5 years primarily because the why was not supported with the how and what. I love bicycles so I'm going to open a bicycle shop. The love does not necessarily mean the market or the consumer requires another bike shop. The why is known and clear but it alone is not enough to sustain a business."*

Sinek's book inspired me to re-brand my business so that I am communicating from the inside out. I want to change the world by helping individuals and organizations reach beyond the status quo – to realize their purpose and deliver their gifts to the world. want to make a real difference in your life and the life of your organization.

Until recently, when people asked what I do, I answered with *what* I do, not *why* I do it. Speaker, trainer, facilitator, consultant, entertainer, these are all what I do. Now, I respond to the same question with something like this; "My purpose in life is to be a change agent and help people and organizations become the best they can be, so they too can change the world and make it a better place (the "why"). My goal is to help organizations become more ***F.I.T.*** by planning for the future, establishing a corporate culture and identity that sets them apart from others, and developing a top notch, cohesive team that provides outstanding customer service (the what). I do this through speaking, training, facilitating, and entertaining (the how)."

Do you see the difference? Customers want to know why you do what you do. Customers want to resonate with your organization's why. When I facilitate a workshop, or present a keynote, I put it all out there. People need to feel that I'm the real deal and someone who can not only help them, but who sincerely wants to.

It doesn't matter what goods or services your organization sells. It's the presentation that makes all the difference. How you treat staff and customers, how you adapt to change or compete in the marketplace, and your authenticity, leadership, and integrity, must all be congruent with the why.

Before we go any further, let's address the elephant in the room. Some of you might be wondering if an organization's why can be to make money. Money is a huge part of our lives. Life is easier with money, and with lots of it one can enjoy the finer things it has to offer. There's no judgment from me about people being in business to make money. That's why I'm in business. If, however, the sole purpose of your organization's why is to make money, and you sacrifice honesty and integrity to get it, you may have a problem.

What do you say when someone asks you what your organization does? Chances are you tell them you sell, create, or provide something. You're probably not telling people *why* you sell, create or provide these things.

Successful Companies Know Their Why

Do you think Facebook is a successful organization? Do you know why Facebook does what it does? Mark Zuckerberg and his pal's initial why was to create a database of dateable women in universities. Since those early days, Facebook has grown way beyond that, even though some people may still use it for its original intent.

Sheryl Sandberg was brought in from Google by Zuckerberg to become Facebook's CEO in 2008. Sandberg has helped Facebook become hugely profitable and in 2012 became the first female to serve on the Board of Directors for the company.

Facebook's popularity is unquestionable. It has provided a way for people to connect in real time from anywhere in the world for free. That's the why. People believe in Facebook. They are loyal to Facebook. Some don't know what they would do without it in their lives. That kind of intense customer loyalty is not easy to find.

Facebook is only one example of an organization whose why is pretty transparent. There are many others. Apple, for example, has a cult-like following that grows larger every day, and I'm proud to say I'm one of them. Have you been to an Apple store? I've never seen so many staff in a store at one time. They're needed to service the huge number of customers that frequent their stores every day.

Why do people like me become Mac users who will never go back to a PC, even though the prices are cheaper, the technology is getting to be just as good, and PCs are most popularly used? Because Mac is cutting edge, thinking outside the box. It's rebellious, it's Steve Jobs. It's Tim Cook, the current CEO, who carries on Job's vision for the company, and who has become the first Fortune 500 CEO to come out as being gay. The reason I mention this is because the leaders at Apple are willing to step outside of the box and make no apologies for who they are, or how they go about their business.

Apple's corporate culture and powerful why has captured the imagination of millions of loyal followers. Sinek says, "People don't buy what you do, they buy why you do it." Don't you want that kind of following for your organization?

How the Airplane Reflects the Why

There's a great story in Sinek's book about Samuel Pierpont Langley and the importance of why. Have you heard of him? Not many have. Langley was one of many who were attempting to become the first human to take flight in an airplane. He was a popular inventor, was well-connected, and every move he made was chronicled by the New York Times. He was granted plenty of money so that he could put together the finest staff to help him succeed.

At the same time Langley was trying to make history, so were Orville and Wilbur Wright. They, however, were unknown, and had no following or patrons to provide them with funds. Still, you probably have heard of the Wright Brothers. That's because they had a powerful why. They felt that if they could invent a machine that could fly, it would change the course of the world. That was the purpose that drove them to never give up. They would make four or five flying attempts each day, but were unshakable in their determination to make it happen.

Langley, on the other hand, simply wanted to be the first, and garner the fame and fortune that would result. When he heard of the Wright Brothers' achievement, he quit. He didn't really care about changing the world. He only cared about getting rich and famous.

Do You Know What Your Why is?

Having, communicating, and building a corporate culture around the why will inspire people. The right people will want to work for you because they're inspired by why you do what you do. The right customers will come and buy because they too will be inspired by your why, and they will remain loyal.

At the beginning of this chapter, I challenged you to ask your employees if they could articulate the why of your organization. An even more fundamental question, now that you have read this chapter, is can *you* articulate the why? Here's my challenge for you.

- Write down, as succinctly as possible, what you believe to be the why of your organization.
- Ask all your employees to do the same.
- Compile the results.

- Determine if you need to have a professional development day to crystallize your why, and to make sure that everyone who works for and with you is on board and going forward together.
- Once you have the why in place, make sure your organizational outcomes (the what), and the how both reflect the why.

When you go through this process, I believe you will create a corporate culture that reflects the purpose of your organization. I believe you will attract the right people to work for you, and the right people to be your customers. I believe that your employees will also be empowered by your why, and be able to conduct business in a much more integral fashion, with clarity and consistency. I believe your customers will remain loyal because they will buy why you do what you do, not what you do. Knowing your why is a great way to help your organization Get ***F.I.T.,*** and Go Far!

CHAPTER TEN

Cultivate Three Essential Qualities Great Organizations Use

The World Needs a Lot More of This

"Be accountable to yourself. Be true to yourself."

-Lailah Gifty Akita

Male Bonding is Alive and Well

There was a time when men gathered around a fire together. They used the opportunity to talk about anything and everything they wanted. They talked about their fears, their women, the hunt, and their dreams. The fire was sacred and it may have been the prequel to Las Vegas, because what was said at the fire, stayed at the fire. There was value in the comfort of hunters coming together to share experiences and supporting each other.

Today, the ritual continues. Some things may have changed, but others have not. We still have the fire and maintain the rule of what happens at the fire stays at the fire, but we have evolved the ritual to include a number of other things. For years I belonged to a men's "tribe" called *Head Smashed In*, named after the nearby World Heritage Site, *Head-Smashed-In Buffalo Jump*.

Much of what we did on our men's team is based on the book *Iron John: A Book About Men* by Robert Bly, who is considered to be the man responsible for inspiring the men's movement in the United States.

The tribe consists of a number of different teams with about ten men on each. The team meets once a week, and yes, we meet around a fire. We have an agenda for a three-hour meeting which includes an activity, a teaching, and a check-in on four pillars of our lives; relationships, spirituality, health, and business/finances.

The check-in is the most important part of the meeting, and when we talk about the four pillars, we open ourselves up to questions and challenges about what we've shared. If we keep bringing the same issue to the fire, men will challenge that. If a man thinks he is ready to get married, he is encouraged to spend time with a group of other married men who will ask a lot of questions to make sure the man knows what marriage is all about.

When we talk about spirituality, we don't talk about religion, but about how each of us connects to a bigger picture whether that is a god or nature or something else. We know that if all four pillars are not strong in our life, we need to do something to get them back in balance. It's not rocket science, but it's amazing how having permission to talk about the way things are in your life empowers you to make the effort to change them.

Calling "Bullshit" with Love and Kindness

When I first heard of this tribe, I was invited to attend a fire. I was amazed by what I witnessed. What I saw was a group of men willing to sacrifice their relationships to each other by being honest with each other. This meant that if you wanted to be in relationship with these men, you had to accept the fact that they would not lie to you when they gave you feedback. No sugar coating, no acceptance of excuses, and no compromises.

They make you take responsibility for your behavior. And, the real kicker for me was that they seemed to do this from a place of love. Imagine knowing that someone loves you enough to call you on your bullshit, to hold you accountable for your behavior no matter what excuses you throw at them, and to offer help and support to meet the challenges that you have difficulty facing alone.

I wanted to be a part of something like that, and joined right after that initial experience. The tribe is part of a larger group of men belonging to an organization called MDI, or Mentor Discover Inspire. The reason I bring up the men's team in this book about organizational fitness is because of what MDI, and the *Head Smashed In* tribe believe. The following excerpt is the MDI vision statement and is taken directly from their website.

"MDI was formed to provide a place for men to learn the principles and practices that enable each man to live a life of honor, become the man he has always wanted to be, and contribute a life well-lived to his family, his fellow man, and his community."

Is there an organization out there that wouldn't think these are good principles? Of course, we're not just talking about men in organizations. These principles apply to all, across the board. I spoke a little about the accountability and honesty factors that are so important, but there is another important component in the mix, and that is integrity.

Living Up to Standards

Our team has standards members are expected to meet. For example, we have to be on time for our weekly meeting, bring wood to the fire, have a phone call with our RAM partner (Respect A Man) up to 24 hours prior to the meeting, and we must return any correspondence from a man on our team within 24 hours. If any of these standards are not met during the week, a man is considered to be "out of integrity." There are many other areas in our life where we could be out of integrity, and we're encouraged to disclose them at the meeting.

One of the biggest issues with organizations is accountability. People talk and make promises without following through, and the end result is mediocrity.

How can an organization be great if they don't follow through on their promises?

If you're out of integrity, you are given an opportunity to cleanup at the meeting. The actions we take for cleanup are not as important as the gesture of performing them. A typical cleanup activity might be twenty pushups, a face wash in a cold river, a three minute cold shower, or running some laps. Once we have cleaned up, we are back in integrity and can be fully present for the meeting.

This opportunity to make amends, to come back into integrity, is so important. As in life, given that second chance can be very empowering. It means that even though we screwed up, we haven't lost value as a human being, or, in the case of an organization, as an employee.

Accountability, honesty, and integrity are the cornerstones of men's teams and also of great leaders and organizations. I think leaders should be transparent, take responsibility for their behavior, admit when they make mistakes, make amends, forgive others for their mistakes, offer honest feedback and support to help colleagues learn and grow, and be accountable to others and for others. Who doesn't want that in their life or in their workplace? If you don't, maybe you shouldn't be a leader. If you do want it, and your organization isn't quite there yet, I have another challenge for you.

One of the biggest issues within organizations is accountability. People talk and make promises without following through, and the end result is mediocrity. How can an organization be great if they don't follow through on their promises or if they fail to take responsibility for being out of integrity?

Have you ever wanted to buy something that was not in stock or had to special order an item, and the staff told you the item would there by a certain day? When the day comes, you expect the item, and it's not there. Sometimes it can be days or weeks later before it arrives. How does this happen and why? How can people make promises they can't keep? Honest mistakes are one thing, as long as we take responsibility for them, but making false promises or not being accountable means we're out of integrity. Do you want to deal with organizations who are out of integrity?

Honesty relates directly to integrity. If you're not honest in the workplace, you can't be in integrity. Not only that, but it requires a tremendous amount of energy to maintain lies. We need to cover them up to keep them going. It's so much easier just to be truthful, even though at times it may bring discomfort or unpleasant consequences. How many stories have we heard in recent years about organizations that have downsized or filed bankruptcy because they had been concealing the truth?

In 2014, a political situation erupted in Alberta in which the leader of the opposition party, along with eight other members of the Legislative Assembly, walked across the floor to join the party in power. This is pretty much an unprecedented move in Alberta politics. What stands out for me is that this opposition leader had been trying to bring down the very government she joined. How can one justify this action and still be in integrity? She has publicly spoken out against the government and has stated that the only way to have change in Alberta is to get rid of them. Now, she is one of them. How do her constituents see this move? As it turns out, she was not re-elected in her riding and has stepped away from political life, at least for the time being.

The Accountability Challenge

Let's get back to my challenge for you. Find an accountability partner, someone in your network of organizational leaders with whom you can share without fear anything related to work, just like we do on our men's team. Your partner can support you, hold you accountable, keep you in integrity, and help you find new ways to provide leadership in your organization.

Meet with your accountability partner at least once a week, either in person or by phone. If you're going to have a phone relationship, I strongly recommend that you also build in face-to-face meetings every once in a while. We can hide more easily on the phone than in person. Choose someone you either don't know at all, but respect, or someone you know a little bit. Do not become partners with someone you know well, because they can be too attached to you to be brutally honest.

The purpose of the partnership is to set professional goals with each other, and then help each other reach them. These goals should be related to developing leadership within your organizations, like a mastermind duo. Don't get too hung up with formalities, but it's a good idea to develop the ground rules at the beginning. Have an agenda and a time limit for meetings and create that agenda together. Keep it open, keep it honest, and give it time.

If you can address these three key components of an organization, honesty, integrity, and accountability, you will grow toward becoming a great leader and making your organization Get ***F.I.T.,*** and Go Far!

T E A M

"With kids, they don't do what you want them to do when you want them to do it. Organizations don't necessarily, either. You've got to listen. You've got to learn how to influence."

-Ellen J. Kullman

How well your team functions

CHAPTER ELEVEN

Build an Unbelievable Team to Lead Your Organization

To Build or Not to Build?

"My model for business is The Beatles. They were four guys who kept each other's kind of negative tendencies in check. They balanced each other and the total was greater than the sum of the parts. That's how I see business: great things in business are never done by one person, they're done by a team of people."

-Steve Jobs

What is Team Building Anyway?

Even though he was known as an autocratic leader, Steve Jobs knew the importance of teamwork. It makes sense that if your team members learn how to accept and utilize their differences they should work more efficiently. Good teamwork though doesn't happen coincidentally. It takes a systematic approach combined with team building activities to create synergistic teams.

Team building activities require time and resources, and you may wonder if the cost of team building outweighs the benefits. How does an organization measure the return on investment (ROI) against the costs of providing team building activities? It's not easy. One way to measure ROI is to track the amount of time spent on assignments before and after team building sessions. If there's a difference in time spent, or more activities are getting done each month than before, that's a good sign the ROI is meaningful.

But is ROI the only reason for providing team building activities in your organization? Let's say the team building sessions create more camaraderie in the workplace, a better overall feeling among staff when they walk in the building. If production or sales aren't going up however, who really cares? Are you, as an employer or manager, willing to spend money and time on building your team if there are no significant changes in sales or productivity?

Before answering that, it's important to realize organizations do lots of things that have nothing to do with ROI. In speaking with a district manager from the Royal Bank of Canada (RBC), I discovered that RBC provides funding for a wide variety of programs, many of which provide no direct ROI. They fund these programs because people in the corporation believe in them. They believe that it's the right thing to do because they are making a difference in the world. Yes, if their name is out there, and someone decides to use RBC as their bank and open an account, then they've gained a customer. But for many programs, that's not their intention.

The question is, do you as an employer think that team building activities are beneficial, from either a ROI point of view, or because it feels like the right thing to do for your organization? The other thing to consider is what do your employees think? If there's conflict in the workplace, mistrust, jealousy, individuality, gossiping, backstabbing, unhealthy competition, and more, are your employees happy with all that going on? Yes, they may be able to work through those things, and still keep up production, but they may be miserable doing so. How will these issues affect the organization in terms of production, or retaining and attracting employees?

When the economy is tough, one of the first budget cuts organizations make seems to be team building activities. Perhaps that's because many organizations define team building as having fun together and, while socializing may be important, it's not a high budget priority, so it gets cut.

Great team building activities however go beyond the social context and help your team learn about each other, their strengths, values, leadership abilities, fears, and weaknesses. Understanding a person brings acceptance and compassion, which can go a long way in getting things done – it's especially helpful in getting through a difficult work day. We're talking about learning to work with each other as a team in the best way to move the organization forward, and that requires more focus than simply having fun together as a group.

Great team building activities that are well planned and debriefed, will help develop leadership skills, foster mutual understanding, create synergy, promote individual nurturing, boost morale, inspire creativity, and generate enthusiasm. What else do you do in your organization in terms of training and professional development that can produce these results all at the same time?

If the purpose of your organization is to ultimately make money, then you need to provide the best customer service possible. Does it make sense then that the more cohesive your team is, the more productive it will be, and therefore more effective and efficient at providing goods and/or services to your customers? Why then would you not want to spend time and money to invest in building your team?

Team building in an organization takes work, time, resources, and intention. If you want to build a great team you need a plan, and to intentionally implement that plan. Without that work and effort, things can become dysfunctional and fall apart.

Never Judge a Book By it's Cover

After completing a Master's Degree in Education, I was hired to be a guidance counsellor in a high school. It's important to note that I was just coming from a 5-year tenure at the democratic style Alternative High School that I talked about in Chapter Seven.

The interview panel was impressed, and assured me that my democratic approach to working with students and staff was what they wanted. They offered me the job and I accepted. On the second day of school, our guidance department had a team meeting, and while there were three counsellors and one assistant on the team, only the counsellors were present. When asked where the assistant was, I was informed by the department head that she wasn't required to attend the meetings. That was big red flag number one.

About two weeks in, during a morning staff meeting, the department head announced that guidance counsellors would be coming into teachers' classes over the coming weeks to do a variety of things. Schedules were passed out indicating what we would be doing in those classes. Neither counsellor was consulted in developing the schedule. Another red flag.

The rest of the school year continued in that non-democratic way. What happened to working together as a team? Was there ever any intention on behalf of the department head to implement democratic methods?

The consequences of these dysfunctional activities were severe. There was a lot of tension in staff meetings and people were afraid to voice their opinions. There was no cohesion amongst the staff. Countless hours and much energy were spent in private conversations talking about what was really going on. There was no trust. Were our "customers" at the school impacted by this dysfunctional team? Of course they were. Staff, students, and parents were all affected by the climate that existed there.

Value Your Team and Great Things Will Happen

Another team I worked with had a much different outcome. At The Keg restaurant, the intention of the management group was to build the best possible team that would serve their customers in the best possible way, thereby insuring longevity for their company. How did they do this?

The Keg incorporated a variety of team building activities into our workday. Everything from social events and sports teams to dynamic training and profit sharing. Beyond the team building activities, there was a feeling that the owners and managers cared about us. They knew that their livelihood depended on us, and how well we worked together.

The Keg knew they had to take care of us, as well as empower us, so that we would fully support what they were selling. One example of this was when the restaurant wanted to test a new product for the menu. They got all their staff to test the new products, and if we didn't like them, they didn't get on the menu. How many organizations do you know operate that way?

The Keg is an example of everything an organization should do. As an employee, I felt valued and appreciated. I felt that the managers had my back and weren't on my back. I felt like I was contributing, along with all the other staff, to making The Keg one of the best restaurants anywhere. That felt really good. I had no such feeling at the high school. I talk more about the Keg Restaurant experience in Chapter Thirteen.

Two organizations, two teams, two sets of intentions for how those teams should be run, and two different ways of engaging staff in the process. Both organizations had team building activities - ones to help bond and have fun, others to train and develop the team. One organization chose to include their staff in the decision-making process for important matters, the other did not. One organization seemed to really care about their staff. The other seemed to only care about some of their staff. Which team would you rather have in your organization?

How Trust Can Make or Break an Organization

At the core of every great team, and in fact, every great organization, there is one component that is essential, and that is trust. Stephen Covey really nailed it when he said, "*There is one thing that is common to every individual, relationship, team, family, organization, nation, economy, and civilization throughout the world - one thing which, if removed, will destroy the most powerful government, the most successful business, the most influential leadership, the greatest friendship, the strongest character, the deepest love. That one thing is trust."*

When I work with organizations, we talk about trust and how the lack of it can erode an organization to the point where everyone is fearful of everyone else, and massive amounts of time and energy are spent trying to create back-room coalitions to provide one with some sense of security. If trust doesn't exist within your organization, you probably already know it. The good news is, you can do something about it. Levels of trust can change by incorporating certain values, systems, and corporate symbols.

When assessing an organization's trust level, I use Covey's four questions as a guide.

How would you describe a low-trust organization?
How would you describe a high-trust organization?
Which description best represents your organization?
What are the results?

In the two examples I shared, the high school would be considered a low-trust organization and The Keg high-trust. In each, there were managerial behaviors that dictated the level of trust, and those behaviors created the corporate culture which impacted staff and customers. Where does your organization lie in terms of the level of trust staff and customers have with it?

Better Teams Bring More Revenue

The last three questions in the Organizational Fitness Test that I gave you in Chapter One are about team. If you scored low points in those questions, there are probably trust issues in your organization. A good way to assess how well you think your team is doing is to go back and review those questions.

One of the great things about team building activities is, if they're done right, trust levels within the organization can change significantly. If trust is a key ingredient in organizational efficiency, and team building activities foster trust among staff, investing in team building activities make sense, regardless of the measurable ROI.

"For every 1 percent improvement in the service climate, there's a 2 percent increase in revenue. Workers who feel upbeat will go the extra mile to please customers, both internal and external, and therefore improve the bottom line."
-Daniel Goleman

If you're still not convinced though, maybe this will help. Research indicates better teams lead to more revenue for an organization. In *Primal Leadership*, Daniel Goleman talks about research on the correlation of organizational climate to productivity in a range of industries. He says, "*For every 1 percent improvement in the service climate, there's a 2 percent increase in revenue. Workers who feel upbeat will go the extra mile to please customers, both internal and external, and therefore improve the bottom line.*"

Here are six ways to build great teams:

- Incorporate activities where your team can bond, socialize, and have fun together.

- Provide activities where your team can share similarities and differences in leadership styles, likes and dislikes, and how they feel about the organization.
- Engage your team in the organizational decision-making process by asking for their feedback. Then make sure to use it.
- In the process to develop your mission statement, make sure *every* employee has bought into the final result.
- Determine the team's level of trust for your organization.
- Ensure the team knows what the organizational goals and values are.

In summary, great organizations need great teams and great teams don't just happen. They require nurturing and attention. They demand time and resources. They require a high level of trust and an opportunity for members to get to know each other in a variety of different ways. Building great teams is a big part of helping organizations Get ***F.I.T.,*** and Go Far!

CHAPTER TWELVE

Six Proven Ways to Engage Employees

Disengaged Employees Cost You Money

"It goes without saying that no company, small or large, can win over the long run without energized employees who believe in the mission and understand how to achieve it."

-Jack Welch

How Engaged Are Your Staff?

You can't have a great team without employees that are engaged. It's important for management to listen to feedback provided by staff. It's also crucial for management to be open to that feedback, and make necessary changes. Staff then feel they are contributing towards bettering the organization. Seeking, accepting, and using staff feedback is one important way to engage your staff.

75% of workers in North America are either not engaged in their work, or actively disengaged.
- Canada Human Resource Center

Just think about how engaged you are in the work that you do. My guess is, if you're not engaged, you're probably wasting a lot of time doing things you're not supposed to be doing, like scrolling Facebook, surfing the net, or even looking for another job. If you are engaged however, you probably bring a fair amount of dedication, determination, and passion to your work, and I'll bet that pays off in terms of how productive you are. What about your employees? What do they bring to the workplace?

According to the Canada Human Resource Center and Gallup polls, many employees in North America are not bringing a whole lot to the workplace. (What the heck are they doing then?) From the chart on the following page, you can see that 75% of workers in North America are either not engaged in their work, or actively disengaged. Not engaged workers are those who come on time, leave on time and essentially put in only the bare minimum at work. By actively disengaged workers, we are talking about employees that are not only unhappy in their work, but they are also spreading that negativity to others in the workplace. You know who those people are in your organization.

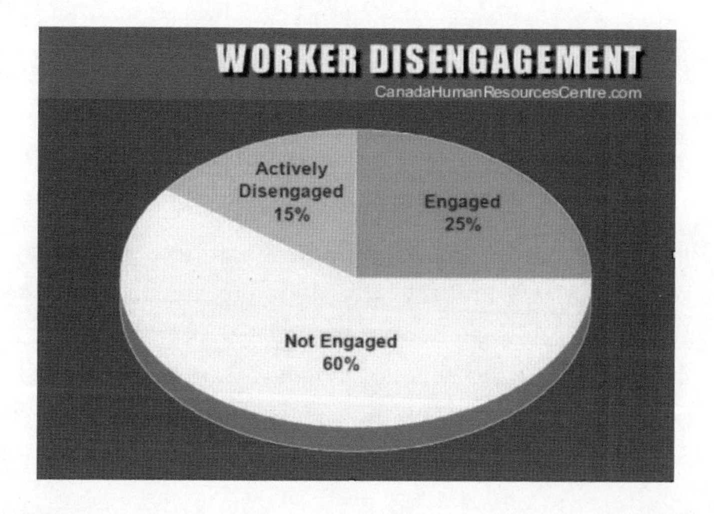

It's the actively disengaged group that also costs organizations the most money in lost productivity. In their article *Disengaged Employees Can Cost the Company Millions,* Kelly Services from Australia presented the results from a five-year study conducted by Gallup. The purpose of the study was to track the cost to organizations of keeping actively disengaged employees on staff. One may ask why organizations even bother to keep these employees around, but it's very difficult sometimes to terminate employees due to collective bargaining agreements. Gallup estimated that the cost to U.S. organizations of keeping these actively disengaged workers on staff was over $300 billion dollars.

Studies on employee engagement also indicate that the higher level people achieve within a company, the more engaged they are. In a study conducted by Towers Perrin in 2003, for example, senior executives were more than twice as engaged in their work as their directors and managers. They were also three times as engaged as the specialists and professionals in the organization, and more than four times as engaged as the hourly workers. From this study, it appears that the further down the organizational hierarchy someone is, the less engaged she will be.

It's quite possible then that you are more engaged in your work than a lot of your employees. What can be done about this? What is the key to employee engagement?

If your organization has ever conducted an internal study on this question, you probably already know the answer. If not, you can easily Google "employee engagement" and come up with hundreds of documents. Or, you can ask people three key questions that will save you thousands of dollars on consultant fees. I share those questions with you at the end of the chapter.

It's Amazing What a Slice of Pizza Can Do

First though, here are two examples of employee engagement that may help you make some changes in your own organization. The first comes from a project I conducted, "Managing Multi-Generations in the Workplace." (I refer to this project in more detail in Chapter Six.) Six different organizations participated in the project and I collected data on what staff and management felt were multi-generational issues in their workplace. From the data, I created a three-hour training workshop, and provided staff with a pre and post-training attitudinal survey to indicate any changes they had about generational issues once the training had been completed.

One of the participating organizations was a large grocery store, and part of a national chain. One of my tasks was to simply walk around and observe. Staff knew who I was and I could blend in rather easily and watch how staff interacted with each other, management, and customers. One day, I noticed a high school employee who was stocking shelves. He appeared to be lethargic, unmotivated, and unhappy.

To create a little conversation, I asked him how he was doing, and then I asked if he was enjoying the task he was required to do. He emphatically said no and that it was boring. One of the things that I learned in my work and research on generational differences, is that generation Y employees usually don't like to work alone. For this young lad, a five-hour shift of stocking shelves on his own like this after a day in school was enough to make him want to die!

The next morning I had a chat with his supervisor, and asked him if he was happy with the work this young lad was doing. He told me that the boy worked very slowly and didn't get a whole lot done. He also said that the boy was a good kid and he didn't want to let him go because of that. The next day, I got his permission to try something different to see if there would be any change in the boy's productivity or demeanor.

At the beginning of the next shift, I got together with the boy, another young male staff, and the supervisor, and asked him to demonstrate exactly how he wanted the shelves to be stocked. I encouraged the boys to watch carefully. When the supervisor was done, I instructed the boys that the one who finishes stocking their shelf first, in exactly the way the supervisor wanted it stocked, gets to go to the deli department and grab a free slice of pizza and a pop.

There was a dramatic difference in the performance of the boy who appeared totally disinterested a day before. This friendly competition created camaraderie, fun, and increased productivity dramatically. More shelves were getting stocked more quickly, and looking much better than ever before. And the cost? Some pizza and pop.

Not only did this intervention make the store look better - and quickly - but it also changed the attitude of those high school students. They were happier at work. Customers who came into contact with them didn't feel the negative energy they may have felt a day earlier. When customers feel good about the energy of a place, it makes them want to shop there and spend money. These two students were now totally engaged.

Empowering Your Staff Pays Off

The second example of employee engagement I want to share with you comes from a Rotary International leadership camp for at-risk youth where I was the director for 12 years. Every year, we brought 65 youth between the ages of 13-18 to a four-day camp to teach leadership skills, trust, and team work. Underlying these objectives was the real purpose of the camp, which was to build self-esteem. The youth who attended the camp were all referred by their school counsellors, and usually because they came from dysfunctional families or weren't doing well in school.

The students were divided into seven groups, and each group had one youth leader and two adult leaders, These 21 volunteer leaders were my staff, and together we planned and executed the curriculum for the four days. We also worked to create an environment that was safe as well as challenging for these youth.

The camp had been running for over twenty years with some amazing success stories. Counsellors, teachers, and parents often commented on what an amazing transformation some of the youth went through in only four days. Many went back to their schools and joined leadership groups or got involved in school culture more than they ever had before. In fact, the youth leaders were all graduates of the camp, and some have since gone on to become adult leaders there.

Why is this camp so successful? In my opinion, it's because everyone is engaged. While I had final say about anything as the director of the camp, I delegated responsibility to everyone as often as I could. We also all agreed that the youth leaders were crucial to the success of the camp because they had gone through it before, and the students were more prone to opening up with people closer to their own age. As a result, we gave the youth leaders enormous responsibility, and they responded beyond our expectations.

When it came time to plan activities for the camp, everyone had a say, and everyone had the opportunity to lead an activity. We used the staff's strengths much more than we ever focused on their weaknesses. Everyone felt like they were a useful part of a team that was doing work that could change people forever.

One wonderful moment was when a youth leader made an important decision that changed a student's life. One of the features at this camp was a zip line, and our goal as leaders was to get our students who had fears around the zip line to conquer those fears and make an attempt at it. Over the years, a number of youth have frozen in fear on the Burma bridge between the two towers before they even got to the zip. When that happens, we do our best to urge the student on, but sometimes we just have to bring them back down.

On this particular day, everyone was inside the main lodge and seated waiting for dinner, except for one of the groups who were still at the zip line. It's traditional that we wait for everyone to finish the activities and eat together, but this was going on too long and I had to make a decision. Just as I was about to do so, the youth leader came into the lodge, informed me that one of the students was frozen on the bridge, and told me that we all needed to go and support him.

Her demeanor was such that I felt compelled to accommodate her request. I made the announcement to the others and all eighty of us went down to the zip line to support this student. The student was overwhelmed by us coming out to support him, and after ten minutes or so, he moved along the Burma bridge to the zip line and came down. When he reached the ground, I have rarely seen such a big smile on anyone's face in my whole life. This was a huge success for him.

I believe strongly that the reason why the youth leader did what she did was because of the responsibility she was given to make decisions and develop her leadership skills. You could only imagine how good that youth leader felt when we all went to support her decision, and it turned out to be the right one.

Three Questions to Determine How Engaged Your Employees Are

As you can see from these two examples, employee engagement is important. If we can reduce the number of not engaged and actively disengaged people, the results in terms of productivity, employee happiness, and customer satisfaction, are well worth the effort it takes. That effort will have a great impact on the bottom line for any organization. It will cost less to produce goods and services, attract and retain higher quality staff, and create greater customer satisfaction over the long term.

What can you do in your organization to begin to address employee engagement? I've given you a couple of examples from my own personal experience, and, as promised, here are the 3 questions you should ask every one of your employees:

1. On a scale of 1-10, how satisfied are you with your job here?
2. What would you like to be doing here that you're not?
3. How can I help?

The important thing to remember with these three questions, or any other type of survey that you conduct in your organization, is that you must be prepared to act on the answers you receive. If you don't, it's simply an exercise in futility and will probably help transform some of your "not engaged" staff to "actively disengaged" staff. It's not that you need to do everything that is suggested in the answers to the questions, but you have to do something.

In addition to those three questions, here are six sure-fire ways to engage your staff:

Value your employees

Show employees that you value them in whatever ways you can. Say thank you, show them respect, offer bonuses, incorporate profit-sharing, or provide extra time off for a job well done.

Prepare your staff to leave

Make sure that there are opportunities in the organization for employees to advance their careers, and if that means their leaving your organization, so be it.

Frequent and immediate feedback

Don't wait for the annual performance review to provide staff with feedback. The feedback should be immediate, it should be honest, and it should be constructive.

Share your vision

It's important that your staff know how their role fits into the big picture of the organization, and therefore why their role is so important in that big picture.

Be ethical

Make sure that you walk the talk - don't expect your staff to do anything that you wouldn't do.

Don't micro-manage

Allow your staff the freedom to fail and to succeed by developing their own decision-making and problem-solving skills.

Take the time and energy necessary to engage your staff. The effort is well worth it and it will lead to your organization becoming more ***F.I.T.***, so it can Go Far!

CHAPTER THIRTEEN

How to Provide Exemplary Customer Service

Would You Be a Customer of Your Own Organization?

"A customer is the most important visitor on our premises, he is not dependent on us. We are dependent on him. He is not an interruption in our work. He is the purpose of it. He is not an outsider in our business. He is part of it. We are not doing him a favour by serving him. He is doing us a favour by giving us an opportunity to do so."

-Kenneth B. Elliott

Do We Expect Good Customer Service?

Having a great team is one thing. Making sure that the team is focused on customer service is another.

Great customer service is something special. Don't you love it when someone goes out of their way to treat you as if you're the only person that mattered in the world? Does your organization provide that kind of exemplary customer service?

Later on in the chapter, I'll share some ways about how to determine the quality of your customer service. The organizational mindset toward customer service starts with the leaders, and filters down. The type of training and supervision staff receive, and the processes that surround serving customers efficiently, are all crucial to providing top quality customer service. As Elliott said in the quote at the beginning of the chapter, there is *nothing* more important than the customer.

Think about your own expectations as a recipient of customer service. Is the kind of customer service you expect the kind that you actually get, or is there a gap between the two? Do you think the quality of customer service has deteriorated over the years, and if so, what factors do you think are contributing to this?

From where I sit, customer service looks to have deteriorated over the years. I feel I am treated to great service less often than in the past, and I've noticed that people seem to care less about providing it. There's an attitude out there that supports mediocrity, and opposes excellence. Not too many people are going the extra mile, and frankly, I think it's the consumer's fault.

We still tip servers for mediocre service in restaurants. We don't complain to managers often enough about poor service or inferior goods. We seem to want to avoid confrontation. It's easier to walk away than to fight and complain. This kind of behavior only perpetuates mediocrity and contributes to declining customer service.

Another contributing factor is a low unemployment rate in a good economy. Jobs become easier to find, so staff don't need to show any loyalty to an organization, and employers don't have time to do in-depth training. In this kind of environment, customer service suffers.

Arm`s Length Customer Service Runs the Risk of Losing Your Mind

Part of the reason we don't confront corporations on their poor products or services is because it's so damn hard to do so! It takes time and an incredible amount of energy to drill through the layers of bureaucracy that organizations create. They claim they have to do this for technological and efficiency reasons. If you believe that, I have some swamp land in Florida that you might be interested in.

My wife and I each have a phone package with a major cell phone provider, and spend a considerable amount of money on those packages. My wife was having problems with her phone, and after taking it to a local kiosk to get assistance, she was told she would have to talk to the customer service department directly.

She subsequently spent countless hours and days, speaking to numerous people, always a different one, re-telling and explaining the story each time. The problem was that each person she talked to failed to identify what my wife was experiencing; anger, frustration, and humiliation. All she wanted was for the company to replace the phone, as it had been fixed, but still wasn't working properly. The company was quoting "policy" and said they could not replace the phone, only repair it. My wife's argument was that they had tried repairing it and that didn't work, so why continue to waste everyone's time when they could easily replace it?

It seemed that no representative my wife was able to talk with was willing or able to do anything other than what was written in policy, regardless of how angry she was. The only reason my wife got any satisfaction in the end is because she is a woman who will not give up, and through research and perseverance, she was finally able to speak to someone who had the power, and chose to use it, to provide her with a new phone.

What's the cost of a cellphone to a major communications provider in this country? How hard would it have been for them to apologize for not repairing the phone properly and offering a new phone right away? How much time and effort would have been saved, and customer goodwill created by doing that?

My wife and I aren't the only ones feeling this downward spiral of customer service. In 2014, American Express conducted a global customer service survey in 10 countries and discovered the following:

Only 33% or less of consumers globally see an increased focus on customer service.
40% of Canadians feel businesses pay less attention to customer service.
25% of consumers globally feel companies miss customer service expectations.

Thankfully, there are many examples of outstanding organizations that provide great customer service. Amazon has been the number one rated company for providing customer service in the United States for five straight years. Hilton, Marriott, and Apple also consistently place in the top ten. In Canada, there's one company in particular that changed my life. I learned everything I needed to know about customer service there, and that has impacted the way I do business today.

Only 33% or less of consumers globally see an increased focus on customer service.

40% of Canadians feel businesses pay less attention to customer service.

25% of consumers globally feel companies miss customer services expectations.
-American Express

Steak Isn't the Only Thing that Sizzles at The Keg

I was very fortunate to have been able to put myself through university by being a waiter at The Keg. The Keg made no bones about the fact that without customers, there was no Keg. This simple, yet crucial realization manifested itself in the day-to-day operations of The Keg in several ways. We did everything in our power to make sure every customer left the restaurant satisfied. This was the company mantra; management demanded it, and fully supported it. Shep Hyken, customer service specialist, sums up this kind of approach to customer service, *"...customer service is not a department you call when you have a complaint. It is a philosophy."*

What a confidence booster for a waiter to know that no matter what a customer complained about, the waiter could offer a solution, monetary or otherwise, and be fully supported by management. When customers are happy, the restaurant makes more money, waiters make more tips, and the world is a better place.

At The Keg, everyone was a part of the team, and everyone knew their role. A great customer experience doesn't happen without the hostess greeting that customer with a smile while showing them to their table, which is clean and ready to go thanks to the bussing staff. The experience continues with a waiter who is friendly, attentive, engaging, and knowledgeable about the menu, the prep staff who spend hours preparing the food before the restaurant opens, the bartenders who are skilled at making any kind of drink, and a cook who truly understands how to present food that looks great and is cooked to perfection.

One of the ways this team concept was illustrated, was by a "tip pool," whereby waiters put 4% of their tips into a pool which was then shared by all the other staff that worked that evening. The amount of money that the support staff received wasn't large, but the theory behind the tip pool was significant. It showed every staff member how important they were to the customer experience.

Even with this great team approach and system, things can go wrong, and they did. But that's another area where The Keg excelled. It didn't matter what the customer complaint was, they were going to fix it. I can't recall any customer leaving the restaurant disenchanted after we worked to fix things by buying their meal, giving them a gift certificate, or doing whatever else we could do to appease them.

The working conditions at The Keg were exceptional. Waiters made great tips, so consequently the support staff made good money via the tip pool. Staff received excellent discounts on food, and the food was fantastic, so why wouldn't we eat there? The Keg also sponsored many kinds of social events. Management knew that keeping their staff happy and working well together was the key to their success.

The Keg slow-pitch team even exemplified great customer service. Everyone loved playing against us. Why? Because we were an upbeat, fun group of folks and we always brought buckets full of margaritas to every game. But we didn't keep those margaritas for just our own players. Every time an opposing player would get a hit or make a great play, one of us would run out to the field and give them a margarita. Now THAT'S customer service!

What about The Keg today? Well, according to *Canadian Business Magazine*, The Keg has 107 restaurants in Canada and the United States, and has made Canada's Top 50 Employers 13 years in a row. In 2015, 85% of its front-line workers report high satisfaction with their jobs and the turnover rate at The Keg is well below industry standards. They must be doing something right.

Don't Forget About Your Internal Customers

The Keg is an example of an organization that truly understands customer service. The most significant aspect of The Keg system to me is the fact that they recognize the importance of their internal customers just as much as they do their external customers. The internal customers are predominately their staff. One of the best ways to determine if your company is successful is to ask your internal customers what they think of it. Do they use your products or services, for example? If not, why? How do they feel about working there? Would they recommend your company to others?

If your internal customers are not on board, chances are you're missing the boat with your external customers as well. Imagine your company with everyone who worked there selling your brand because they love going to work for you and believe in your products and services. Here I am, talking about and recommending The Keg thirty years after I worked there. They sure had an impact on me.

There's another level of internal customers though that goes beyond your immediate staff. It's all the people your organization does business with; your suppliers, bankers, lawyers, accountants, and couriers. All of these people are potential customers. If you treat them the same as someone who is actually buying your product and service, you are building relationships with them, and they may eventually become paying customers.

Creating a great relationship with all of your internal customers helps the organization run more smoothly and take care of its external customers. Scott Miller, VP of Kirk Miller & Associates, said that internal customer service is the *"...primary path to exceptional customer service."* The internal customer stream is one that many organizations overlook.

If You're Not Here to Serve Customers, Then Why are You Here?

One of the things I notice in my consulting work is that customers are sometimes taken for granted, and when that happens, it can affect the whole culture of the organization. I was facilitating a training event with the staff at an aquatic center. At one point during the session, we were talking about customer service, and some of the lifeguards were complaining about a number of senior citizens who come into the center and are so "demanding." The staff went on to say that these folks are always asking for things and behave rudely if you don't get it for them right away.

I listened for a while and then asked the staff to tell me what was written on the sign that was underneath the registration desk. Not one of them could tell me, not even the manager. The sign reads, "*You, our customer, are the only reason we are here!*" If the center really believed this, and their focus really was on their customers, I'm pretty sure the discussion during that training session would have been quite different.

Does Great Customer Service Actually Pay Off?

It never ceases to amaze me how many companies I come into contact with that don't understand customer service. Most problems that occur in organizations revolve around customer service (both internal and external) in some way. When organizations are having difficulty attracting and retaining staff, they need to look at how they treat their internal customers, and how they engage their staff. If they're having difficulty with cash flow, they need to examine their products and services. Finally, if an organization is not getting a lot of repeat business, it's either because of the value and quality of the product or service they sell, or the way they treat their customers.

Does great customer service pay off? Of course it does. In that same American Express study I mentioned, they found that 60% of global consumers spend more money with a company that provides them with great customer service experiences. In Canada and the United States, that figure climbs to the 75% range. And those 75% of consumers will spend 12-14% more dollars with those businesses that provide great customer service. Imagine 75 out of every 100 of your customers spending 12-14% more money in your business. Not only that, more than 40% of your customers who receive great customer service will tell others.

On the other hand, poor customer service can lead to lost sales. American Express reports that more than 50% of consumers globally did not complete a transaction or make an intended purchase because of poor customer service. In Canada and the United States, about 35% of consumers will immediately switch companies after a bad customer service experience.

So how do you know if your organization provides great customer service? Here are some ways you can find out:

Ask your external customers how they feel about your service

This may seem obvious but when I was working with a large urban school board's IT department, I asked them what evidence they had to reflect how their customers (schools) felt about their service. They had none. They'd never asked.

Ask your internal customers how they feel about your service

Internal customers are critical to the company's success. They also need to be asked how they feel about your goods and services, whether or not they would buy them, and whether or not they would recommend your company to others.

Check out social media reviews

More and more people check social media reviews basing their purchasing decisions on testimonials. It's crucial to keep on top of those reviews and make comments on the negative ones as to how you will address the concern that a consumer has brought up.

Allow customers to complain

If you don't have a customer complaint process in place, develop one. Then, monitor the level and types of complaints and take steps to rectify them. Thank customers for providing you with feedback that will help make your organization stronger.

Finally, here are 10 tips on how to provide great customer service:

- Deliver value for your goods and services.
- Make it easy for customers to do business with you - in person, and online.
- Whenever possible, deal with your customers face-to-face.
- Make it easy for customers to find out information about products and services.
- Provide a personalized service.
- Make sure customers can speak to someone who is knowledgeable.
- Thank your customers.

- Ask your customers about their experience with you.
- Be efficient when handling customer problems.
- Be courteous.

Customer service is the key to success for any organization. When I used to work in the education system, I recall sarcastic comments in staff rooms like "*If it wasn't for these damn students and parents, we'd be able to get some work done around here!*" Don't ever let it get to this point in your business. Honor your customers. Treat them with respect. Provide them with outstanding service, the kind you want when you're a customer. After all, they truly are the only reason we are here. Great customer service will indeed help an organization Get ***F.I.T.,*** and Go Far!

CHAPTER FOURTEEN

Use SMART Goals and Difficult Conversations to Improve Performance

Making Performance Reviews a Positive Experience

"The best way to inspire people to superior performance is to convince them by everything you do and by your everyday attitude that you are wholeheartedly supporting them."

-Harold S. Geneen

What Makes a Good Performance Review?

One of the best ways to build a team is to make sure there is great communication between staff and management.

My experience as a consultant has taught me some valuable things. One of the things I've learned is that there are some very different approaches to handling performance management reviews (PMRs). I've encountered a number of organizations that are unhappy with the process and the results. In some cases, managers and employees would rather contend with a pit of rattlesnakes than endure a PMR.

Why is that? People seem to dread an upcoming review. Employees aren't sure what will happen, and expect the worst. In this state of fear, employees spend less time on work because they're worrying about the review so much. Management tends not to like them either because they seem more like an exercise in processing paperwork than having any real impact.

Where do you stand when it comes to PMRs? Does your organization use them? Are you for or against them? Have you modified them to meet the needs of both staff and management?

When there is reluctance on both sides in an organization to have PMRs, I wonder why they are used in those organizations. I think we need them. It's important that we constantly monitor performance to see what's working, what isn't, and what we need to improve on.

Some of the models out there though are downright dangerous in my opinion. They're dangerous because they create a one-sided snapshot of how someone (the boss) perceives an employee's performance, and are used to determine promotion and wage increases. There's a lot at stake with these performance reviews. They can also be unproductive because, if they're set up in an adversarial way, i.e. *"you need to perform better or you won't get a promotion,"* it becomes a barrier to honest communication.

Employees tell bosses what they want to hear to get through the review and keep their job. If there has been any situation between reviews where employees wanted to give their boss feedback about how they're being treated, they instead hold their tongues. Sound familiar?

What makes a good PMR? If your organization is conducting just one PMR per year, stop it! I recommend at least four. When you have only one review a year, it's virtually impossible to remember what happened eleven months ago even if the documentation of the event was good. The long gap between reviews also means staff aren't getting patted on the back as often as they should because things go unnoticed until review time.

Feedback between employees and managers needs to happen regularly, and it needs to go both ways. Staff should be able to provide performance feedback to their supervisors without fear of retribution. Are you willing to do that? Do you realize what an effect that will have on the staff/management relationship if you would receive and address the feedback your subordinates gave? Showing vulnerability is a huge asset in building relationships with people. This feedback can be given during informal conversations throughout the year, in addition to the four formal PMRs. This way, both positive and negative behavior is dealt with as soon as possible.

From the Front Line to the Front Office

A fire department in an urban center asked me to come and work with a group of their senior managers to help them prepare for a new performance management model they were implementing. They wanted me to teach these managers how to be coaches for their staff so that the PMR would look more like a coaching session rather than a formal evaluation session. The fire department felt that traditional performance reviews didn't work well for them, and they wanted to try something different.

I learned two important things from the experience. First, a number of the senior managers were concerned because they had been promoted recently, without much training on how to be a manager. They had just left the front line and were having difficulty communicating with their staff from a supervisory point of view. They were now the boss instead of a buddy, and didn't know quite how to handle it.

This brings up the whole notion that just because you are a good front line worker doesn't mean you should be promoted to become a manager. This is a flaw in the traditional performance review model. If you're evaluated as a good firefighter, in this case, you get a promotion to become a team leader, whether or not you have any real leadership skills. There's a disconnect here.

The same disconnect applies in the world of education. Those evaluated as good teachers get promoted to be administrators, and sometimes they are terrible at it. We need to find better ways to develop leaders other than promoting them from within the ranks based on their performance as a front line worker. We need to change that aspect of the PMR.

What I see happening to many folks who are thrust into leadership positions without the proper preparation, is that they don't want to give up their position, and don't want to go back, regardless of how poorly they are adapting to the situation. They don't want to feel like they have failed. They also don't want to give up the money and prestige that comes with a management role. This brings up the important question of how we develop leadership within organizations, particularly through PMRs, and just how qualified our managers/supervisors are to do a good job.

Not Everyone Sets SMART Goals

The second important thing I learned from the fire department gig was that these senior managers didn't know how to set clear goals. In performance reviews, the idea is to set clear goals for staff to follow, and then evaluate how they did in terms of meeting those goals. I was surprised by this fact until I observed other managers doing the same thing. They didn't know how to set clear goals either.

In working with the firefighters, I offered them two tools to help them with goal setting and having difficult conversations with staff, whether it be at PMR time, or just in general. First, I introduced them to the SMART goal-setting model. This is an excellent tool when writing out goals for job descriptions and PMRs.

The SMART acronym stands for:

S Specific
M Measurable
A Attainable
R Relevant
T Timely

If your goal doesn't meet these criteria, then it isn't a SMART goal and you may want to re-think it. For example, one of the things firefighters have to be evaluated on is how quickly they can leave the station ready to fight a fire after the fire alarm rings. In their performance review criteria, they had a goal statement which went something like this; *Fire trucks and all personnel will be ready to respond to a fire within 90 seconds of an alarm.*

The fire department thought this was a good goal statement. But if you apply the SMART model to it, is it specific? There are different ways to interpret "will be ready". If every firefighter doesn't have the same interpretation of that phrase, some may not be "ready" when the alarm sounds.

What's needed in that goal statement is to be specific about what being ready means. There is a list of things that a firefighter needs to wear and have with them in order to be ready, and there is a list of things that must be done to make sure the fire truck is ready. After the training, the statement now reads something like this; *All personnel will have themselves and the appropriate vehicles ready, according to pages 23 and 27 of the Firefighter's Manual, to respond to a fire within 90 seconds of an alarm.*

This subtle change makes the goal that much more SMART, and when a senior manager is evaluating the goal, he can easily measure it. If the goals in your organization are not SMART, they may leave room for ambiguity when it comes time to evaluate performance related to those goals.

If Something is Bothering You About a Staff Member, You Need to Talk About It

Having difficult conversations with staff was another skill that many of these firefighters lacked. While they agreed the conversations were necessary, they wanted to avoid them, likely because they were not trained on how to conduct them. The conversations that we're talking about could happen during the PMR, but more likely they are conversations that should happen informally as well when a situation needs to be dealt with.

When having a difficult conversation with a staff member, it's important to consider what the manager wants the outcome of the conversation to be. If the outcome is to have the subordinate do what the manager wants them to do, that's going to have an impact on the way the conversation goes. If the outcome however, is to discuss how one's actions can put other people in danger when procedures aren't followed, that's an entirely different kind of conversation.

It's also important for the manager to consider what type of relationship outcome he wants with the staff member. Do they want an open and honest relationship where both parties speak about their feelings and what they are experiencing, or do they want the relationship to be strictly supervisor/subordinate? If we set our intention to have certain outcomes when we have conversations with people, those conversations become more effective.

Another key to having difficult conversations with staff is knowing when and how to give feedback. It's surprising to me how many managers don't know how to give good feedback. It's often judgmental, and not descriptive. "Great job" means nothing unless one describes what it is that was done that one considers to be great. Instead of saying, "great job" why not say something like, "*I thought you did a great job today when you communicated to the men that the fire had reached a point where it was no longer safe for them to enter the building. That quick assessment may have saved some lives.*"

Most of us want and need feedback. Our egos like it when someone tells us we're doing great but without that descriptive component we may never actually know what it is that we're doing great, so it becomes difficult to achieve or excel. Negative feedback has to be even more descriptive sometimes, because if we're trying to eliminate a behavior, we better be able to describe what that behavior is.

Here's a 5-Step process for having difficult conversations:

Prepare

Make sure that the person you're going to have the conversation with is involved in setting the time and day for the meeting. The person should know what the meeting is for, but you need to be careful not to plan it too far in advance because the employee could agonize over what will take place. At the same time, asking for a meeting on the spot is not a good idea, so set a time and date that's suitable for both parties. In terms of your own preparation for that meeting, know your intended outcomes as mentioned before. How do you want the relationship to be at the end of the meeting, and what do you want to see happen as a result of the conversation?

Point

Once the meeting starts, get to the point. Don't ask about the family or sugar coat the meeting in any way. Get to the point. People know when they're being set up by flattery or small talk. These conversations are not designed for that. When we're open and direct it may be a bit of a shock at first, but they will quickly get over that.

Link

It's highly important to link the conversation to the bigger picture. This is a crucial point, because if the supervisor is providing feedback based on their opinion of what's wrong, that's not enough. It has to be based on something beyond a personal feeling or observation. The behavior that the manager wants to correct must connect with company standards. This removes the adversarial element, and keeps the conversation more objective.

Plan

Once the behavior that needs to be changed has been discussed and agreed upon, there needs to be a plan put into place to rectify that behavior, a SMART goal if you will. It's really important here for the employee to determine, as much as possible, what that plan is going to be.

Follow-up

Finally, there needs to be follow up. If the plan has a timeline of thirty days, make sure you have another conversation in thirty days to determine if there has been any change in behavior, what that change is, and whether or not another plan needs to be put in place.

PMRs are necessary in any organization. How they are conducted though is the key. The traditional, once a year PMR is slowly going the way of the dinosaur. A number of organizations are not even calling the evaluation a PMR anymore, but instead refer to it as a Performance and Development Review (P&DR). The shift in language is significant because it implies that there is a plan to develop an employee's skills along the way. Developing leadership skills, for example, to prepare front line workers for management positions would be included in the plan leading to this type of review.

Any goals set for the employee to complete before the next P&DR must be agreed to by both parties. This way, the employee buys in and feels the goals are achievable. Other aspects of the organization like promotion, wage increases, career development opportunities, and probationary periods, must all be thoroughly understood by the employee through these P&DR sessions. Another good strategy is for employees to communicate their progress on the P&DR plan prior to the meeting, so that employers can prepare more adequately with current information.

Here are five recommendations for successful Performance & Development Reviews:

- Conduct formal sessions every three months, and informal ones as needed.
- Use SMART goals so that everyone is clear on what needs to be done.
- Give descriptive feedback so people know where they stand with their performance.
- Use the 5-step process to have difficult conversations with your staff.
- Make sure staff buy into the plan.

Implementing great performance & development reviews will indeed help your organization become more ***F.I.T.,*** and Go Far*!*

CHAPTER FIFTEEN

How to Make Fearless Decisions Every Time

Our Gut Brain is Smarter than We Think

"Whenever you see a successful business,
someone once made a courageous decision."

-Peter F. Drucker

What Kind of Decision Maker Are You?

Every great team usually has great leaders, and one aspect of great leadership is making fearless decisions.

How many decisions do you make every day? The answer would depend on what you consider to be a decision. For example, when you wake up in the morning and turn on a light, is that a decision? If you search the internet you will find articles out there that suggest we make up to five thousand decisions a day. I'm already tired.

Of course, many of the decisions we make each and every day are habitual like brushing our teeth, or taking a certain route to work. But let's instead focus on the decisions that have significant consequences in both our personal and professional lives.

> *If you search the internet you will find articles out there that suggest we make up to five thousand decisions a day.*

Consequences for the decisions we make can impact our lives and the lives of people around us. There is a lot riding on the decisions you make, so it's best to figure out ways to make great decisions to keep you and your organization on track.

First, it's important to reflect on the kind of decision maker you are, particularly as relates to organizations. Here are four kinds of decision makers.

Democratic Decision Maker

The democratic decision maker gives up control and invites the group to participate in the decision making process. It's about putting things to a vote and having the majority rule. The advantages are that the group can come to a quick decision, and that there is group participation. The big disadvantage of this decision making style is that there is no one person who is responsible for the decision. In fact, you may find that if the decision doesn't work out, some might say, "Well I didn't vote for that!"

Autocratic Decision Maker

The autocratic decision maker has total control and responsibility for the decision being made, no matter what the outcome. In this type of decision making, the leader doesn't usually ask for, or use any outside information. The advantages are that a decision can be made quickly, there is someone who is responsible for the outcome, and in emergency situations, this might be the best decision making style, because time is of the essence. The disadvantages include employees feeling left out, a lack of effort from employees if they disagree with the decision, and if an employee is directly affected by the decision, but not included in the process, there could be a drop in morale. Leader credibility can also be affected if the decision is questionable.

Participative Decision Maker

The participative decision maker involves others in the process by asking their opinions and perspective, but making the final decision and taking full responsibility for the outcome. The advantages include participation from others, and when a decision directly affects an employee, that employee is involved and has some input. The big disadvantage of this decision making style is that it can take longer because so many people are involved.

Consensus Decision Maker

The consensus decision maker gives up total control of the decision making process. The entire organization is now responsible for the decision. It's different than the democratic model because everyone in the organization must agree and buy in to the decision. If total agreement is not possible, then the decision becomes democratic, and it's put to a vote. Advantages to this style include; getting everyone involved, making a more accurate decision because so many perspectives and ideas have been included, and a higher degree of success. The disadvantages of this style are that it takes a long time to come to a decision, and it requires great skill to include everyone equally in the process.

Where are you in this spectrum of decision making? Perhaps you use a little of each style or change your method depending on the situation. Do you use a specific decision making model when you make important decisions? How successful are you with the decisions that you make? How do some of the world's organizational gurus make decisions and how successful are they?

How Do Celebrities Make Decisions?

From what I've read, Steve Jobs was an autocratic decision maker. He relied entirely on his instincts and he didn't really give a damn about what other people thought. What was so special about Jobs though, is that he could get away with that kind of decision making behavior, because his vision was so incredibly clear to him and so unique to the rest of us. Jobs was essentially a dictator though, and while he got things done, he left a path of destruction in his wake.

If you read up on Oprah Winfrey, you'll find that her most important decisions in life were also made by instinct, or her gut feeling. She talks about her decision to retire from the Oprah Winfrey Show, for example, as one that came entirely from her instinct. Oprah doesn't seem to have as dictatorial a reputation as Steve Jobs does, but she certainly gets things done, and uses her instincts to drive her.

Wal-Mart's founder, Sam Walton, had a different way of making decisions. He created a culture at Wal-Mart in which he called all his employees associates and he empowered them to make a lot of the day-to-day decisions in the organization. He wanted them to take ownership of the business, and in doing so expected they would feel more connected to the organization, be more loyal, and go out of their way to provide outstanding customer service. However, Sam Walton created this culture in his organization because his gut told him that was the best way to run a company.

Are you seeing a pattern here? Instinctual decision making is at the core of three of these famous and successful entrepreneurs who have changed the world. There are many more examples of organizational leaders who make decisions this way. Why doesn't everyone? If the point of decision making is to make the best decision, minimize negative consequences, and optimize positive results, what gets in the way?

If You Have *FEP*, and You Probably Do, it May Kill You

FEP kills. And we ALL have it. FEP stands for; fear, ego, and pride. I think most bad decisions are made because one of these three things gets in the way.

Fear is defined by the Oxford Dictionary as "*an unpleasant emotion caused by the threat of danger, pain, or harm*" *and* "*to avoid doing something because one is afraid.*" Have you ever made decisions in your life and in your business to avoid danger, pain, or harm, or because you were afraid of something? I know I have.

When I finally got into university as a mature student, I felt I was ready for post-secondary education. I knew I wanted to be a teacher. When it came time to make a decision about what kind of teacher, I spoke to academic advisors at the university and researched the labor market. Everything pointed to me becoming an elementary reading specialist. Why? There were very few males in that field at the time, and I was assured of finding a job upon graduation. I was not excited about becoming an elementary school reading specialist, nor was I crazy about little kids, but I was afraid of not being able to find a job when I was done.

After signing up for the courses I needed, within weeks I was bored, frustrated, and dreading classes. I hated the course work so I knew I was going to hate the actual job. My fear-based decision had not been a good one. Thankfully, I adjusted my course and chose differently out of desire, not fear.

How many people do you know, including yourself, who have made decisions out of fear, and did not alter their path despite the consequences of their decision? Many people hate their current work but refuse to change because of fear. Surveys show that over fifty percent of the working adults in North America hate their job. Are you one of those people? Are any of your staff?

Ego is defined in the Oxford Dictionary as "a *person's sense of self-esteem or self-importance.*" When ego is being attacked, feelings of alienation, resentment, and inferiority surface. When that happens, it's no wonder that we make decisions without total clarity of thought. Decisions made to protect ego will often create the very same feelings of alienation, resentment, and inferiority that we felt when our ego was attacked. These decisions are not conducive to moving organizations forward.

Pride is defined in the Oxford Dictionary as "a *feeling of deep pleasure or satisfaction derived from one's own achievements, the achievements of one's close associates, or from qualities or possessions that are widely admired.*" Pride is even considered to be one of Catholicism's seven deadly sins.

A few years ago, I created a CD of original music. I spent a lot of time and money on the project and I take great pride in it. When I first put out the CD, I was amazed and disappointed that no one in my family asked to buy one or download the music. After a year or so of resenting them for that, I decided to surrender and just give them a copy. Again, to my amazement and disappointment, not one of them made any comments about the CD. Now I have given away and sold hundreds of these CDs, and have received numerous unsolicited accolades for it, but none from my family. How did this resentment manifest itself in my life? It made me think twice before saying or doing something nice for one of my family members. This awareness of how pride affects my decision making has matured me in how I interact with my family.

The point of bringing *FEP* into the conversation is to illustrate how our emotions affect the decisions we make. So how do you make fearless decisions that are the right ones?

Here are seven tips on making great decisions:

Your purpose dictates your decisions

If you haven't figured out your purpose in life yet, or why your organization exists, then it's time you did. With a purpose and a why, every decision must measure up to and reflect the standards of that purpose.

Don't let *FEP* get in your way

As mentioned, *FEP* will kill us, if we let it. The only way to stop *FEP* is to be aware of when we're afraid, and when our pride or ego is feeling attacked. Always check those big decisions to see if *FEP* is behind them.

Be a sponge and soak up what you need to know

There's no harm in gathering all the data you need to make an informed decision about something. Then get input from others to help you make the decision.

Use your network

Once you've made a decision, share it with a trusted friend or colleague to see how it sits with them. Sometimes we're so caught up in our own lives that we can't see the forest for the trees. Having an objective opinion will really help.

Trust your intuition

This is the big one folks. This is how Steve Jobs, Oprah, Sam Walton, and many others got as far as they did. They trusted their intuition no matter what. Even after you have gathered information, consulted others, and weighed the pros and cons, the bottom line is that you have to trust yourself.

Never look back

Once the decision is made, don't look back regardless of the outcome. It's a waste of time, energy, and resources to regret making a decision. You have to keep moving forward. Learn what you can from the situation and move on.

If you really, really can't decide, flip a quarter!

Brian Lee, speaker, author, and entrepreneur, shared this little tidbit with me about the quarter flip. You're down to two options and just can't decide. Should you take the red pill or the blue pill? Assign one option to heads and the other to tails. Then flip the coin but catch it before it lands. The theory is that psychologically we will assign the option we really want (our intuition or gut feeling) to heads. It doesn't matter then what would have happened when the quarter hit the ground. Your decision was already made.

Organizations need leaders that consistently make great, fearless decisions. These great decisions will help move the organization forward, build staff cohesiveness, and foster outstanding customer service. All important factors for an organization to Get *F.I.T.*, and Go Far!

ABOUT THE AUTHOR

Born in Montreal, Herky has developed a passion for helping people and organizations identify barriers, develop skills to remove those barriers, and move towards personal and organizational fitness.

His wife Riesah Prock says the reason Herky has developed such passion for this work is because he himself is a misfit. Herky doesn't always like to admit his wife is right, but in this case she is.

At 3 years old, rather than fit in at a family barbecue, Herky snuck away to row his family's boat out into the middle of the lake, much to the family's chagrin when they discovered him missing. When he was 8, he quit school for the first time (2 more times after that) because he was being bullied for being fat and having a weird name (go figure). In high school, he always felt like he was on the outside looking in. He wasn't popular with the girls and wasn't great at sports In fact, Herky wasn't good at anything really, including school. He was just kind of there. ... and the list goes on.

How Can a Misfit Cope?

Herky has developed a variety of skills to set him apart from others so that he could be noticed, skills such as; leadership, public speaking, facilitating, listening, creativity, observation, analysis, performing/writing music, and humor. Ironically, these skills that were developed to get noticed and stand out, also allow him to fit more easily into society. Now he is very comfortable in social situations, is accepting of others, and at ease with people from all walks of life.

Another interesting outcome of being a misfit is that Herky has developed a sixth sense when it comes to working with people and organizations. His keen instinct enables him to perceive issues that others can't see, and identify how to address them.

From early on, his dad's advice had been that it wasn't the job title that mattered, but how well the job was done. That sage advice impacted Herky's life and career from his start at age twelve as an entrepreneur with a paper route, all the way to now.

Today, Herky focuses on organizational fitness and development, bringing a wealth of experience from his background in business, education, and career development. His years and experience have taught him that fitting in is not necessarily a good thing, nor is being a misfit bad. Organizational fitness has less to do with people fitting in and maintaining the status quo, and more to do with developing skills and attitudes that move the organization forward.

Herky has a Bachelor's Degree in Education, a Master's Degree in Human Resources Administration specializing in Organizational Development, and is a certified teacher, speaker and career development professional. He has been in private practice since 1992.

Herky currently lives with his wife Riesah Prock outside of beautiful Waterton Lakes National Park in Southern Alberta. He enjoys hiking, canoeing, swimming, movies, taking risks, and performing as a solo musician.

REFERENCES

Chapter One

Buckingham, Marcus, Coffman, Curtis, *First Break All the Rules: What The Worlds Greatest Managers Do Differently*, Simon & Schuster, 1999

Mary Pickford quote, https://www.goodreads.com/author/quotes/527606.Mary_Pickford

Chapter Two

Bill Drayton quote, http://www.brainyquote.com/quotes/quotes/b/billdrayto542693.html

Lyrics from "Changes," songwriter David Bowie, published by Lyrics © BMG RIGHTS MANAGEMENT US, LLC , Sony/ATV Music Publishing LLC, TINTORETTO MUSIC

De Geus, Arie, *The Living Company: Habits for Survival in a Turbulent Business Environment*, Harvard Business School Press, 2002

"The World's Most Ethical Companies," ethisphere.com, http://ethisphere.com/worlds-most-ethical/wme-honorees/

Eckhart Tolle quote, http://simplereminders.com/quotes/changes-look-negative-something-new-emerge.html

Chapter Three

Morris Chang quote, http://www.missvinc.com/without-strategy-execution-is-aimless-without-execution-strategy-is-useless-morris-chang-ceo-tsmc/

Shankar, Shyama, "Strategic Planning," Management Guru, Mar. 24, 2014, http://www.managementguru.net/strategic-planning/

Chapter Four

Sivaprakash Sidhu quote, http://www.goodreads.com/quotes/4277714-investing-time-to-learn-something-in-your-professional-make-you

Silverman, Rachel Emma, "So Much Training, So Little to Show for It," Wall Street Journal, October, 2012, http://www.wsj.com/articles/SB1000142405297020442590457807295051858328

Chapter Five

Charlotte Beers quote,
http://www.goodreads.com/quotes/1224268-being-in-charge-of-your-work-life-doesn-t-mean-you

Stewart, Nicole, "Missing in Action: Absenteeism Trends in Canadian Organizations," Conference Board of Canada, 2013, http://www.conferenceboard.ca/e-library/abstract.aspx?did=5780

Irene Rosenfeld quote, http://www.brainyquote.com/quotes/quotes/i/irenerosen520466.html

Chapter Six

George Orwell quote, http://www.brainyquote.com/quotes/quotes/g/georgeorwe189106.html

Lyrics from "Respect," songwriters Otis Redding, Anquette Allen, published by Lyrics © Warner/Chappell Music, Inc., Universal Music Publishing Group

Chapter Seven

John Quincy Adams quote, http://www.brainyquote.com/quotes/quotes/j/johnquincy386752.html

Goleman, Daniel, "Leadership That Gets Results," Harvard Business Review, March,2000, https://hbr.org/2000/03/leadership-that-gets-results

Hill, Linda, "Leading from Behind," Harvard Business Review, May, 2010, https://hbr.org/2010/05/leading-from-behind/

Teddy Roosevelt quote, http://www.phrases.org.uk/meanings/speak-softly-and-carry-a-big-stick.html

Chapter Eight

Louis V. Gerstner quote,
http://www.azquotes.com/quote/706434

Lyrics from "I'd Like to Teach the World to Sing," songwriters, Bill Backer, Roger Cook, Roger Greenaway, Roquel Davis, published by Lyrics © SONY ATV MUSIC PUB LLC

"Corporate Culture" definition, Small Business Encyclopedia, Entrepreneur Magazine

"Circle of Courage©," Reclaiming Youth International, https://www.reclaiming.com/content/aboutcircleofcourage

Chapter Nine

Sinek, Simon, *Start With Why: How Great Leaders Inspire Everyone To Take Action*, Penguin Publishing Group, 2011

Chapter Ten

Lailah Gifty Akita quote, http://www.goodreads.com/quotes/1348689-be-accountable-to-yourself-be-true-to-your-self

Bly, Robert, *Iron John: A Book About Men*, Da Capo Press; Reprint edition (July 28 2004)

Ellen J. Kullman quote, http://www.azquotes.com/author/29685-Ellen_J_Kullman

Chapter Eleven

Steve Jobs quote, http://www.goodreads.com/quotes/622900-my-model-for-business-is-the-beatles-they-were-four

Covey, Stephen M.R., *The Speed of Trust: The One Thing That Changes Everything,* Free Press, 2008

Goleman, Daniel, Primal Leadership: Realizing the Power of Emotional Intelligence, Harvard Business School Press, 2002

Chapter Twelve

Jack Welch quote, http://www.frontstream.com/30-inspirational-employee-engagement-quotes/

"Employee Engagement," Canada Human Resources Center, http://www.canadahrcentre.com/solutions/employee-engagement/

"Disengaged Employees Can Cost The Company Millions," Smart Manager, Kelly Services, http://kellyglobal.net/eprise/main/cms/content/au/smartmanager/en/pages/disengaged_employees_cost_millions.html

"Working Today: Understanding What Drives Employee Engagement," Towers Perrin Talent Report, 2003, http://www.keepem.com/doc_files/Towers_Perrin_Talent_2003(TheFinal).pdf

Chapter Thirteen

Kenneth B. Elliott quote, http://www.goodreads.com/quotes/128116-a-customer-is-the-most-important-visitor-on-our-premises

"Global Customer Service Barometer," American Express, 2014, http://about.americanexpress.com/news/docs/2014x/2014-Global-Customer-Service-Barometer-US.pdf

Hyken Shep, "Internal Customer Service," Shep Hyken's Customer Service Blog, http://hyken.com/customer-service-3/1117/

Miller, Scott, "Internal Customer Service: Getting Your Organization to Work Together," Entrepreneur, May, 2002, http://www.entrepreneur.com/article/51804

"Canada's Best Employers," Canadian Business Magazine, 2015, http://www.canadianbusiness.com/lists-and-rankings/best-jobs/2015-best-employers-top-50/

Chapter Fourteen

Harold S. Geneen quote, http://www.brainyquote.com/quotes/quotes/h/haroldsge150857.html

Chapter Fifteen

Peter F. Drucker quote,
http://www.goodreads.com/quotes/451403-whenever-you-see-a-successful-business-someone-once-made-a

Printed in Canada